About the Author

Kenny Maule was born on the Ayrshire coast, and at the age of ten his family brought him to St Ives, Cornwall in 1961. He began learning to surf when surfing in the UK was very new, introduced by Australians. Whilst at uni, he escaped every summer for four years to be a lifeguard at Sennen Beach, near Land's End. Again, this was a new endeavour as professional lifeguards were just beginning. He graduated from the University of Southampton with a BSc (maths) in 1972 and spent six months as a teacher in Barbados and three months hitch-hiking through the USA, Canada, Alaska, then overland to Popayan in the Andes of Colombia, spending a year overseas.

Deciding the oceans were big but not big enough, and anyway the skies were even bigger, he sloughed off his previous escapism and learnt to fly with BA. Kenny has 'lived a bit' as a pilot flying worldwide and working as an instructor and examiner whilst residing in China, France, Switzerland, India, Russia, and Australia on V.I.P., Airbus, and Boeing aircraft.

Born on the Scottish coast, growing up on the Cornish coast, he has worked almost everywhere in the world and in all cultures. Like all 'good' pilots, he is divorced and remarried with two adult children from the first marriage and two adult children from the second marriage, plus increasing numbers of grandchildren. Living over the harbour of a North Sea fishing port, there's just enough time to scribble his enduring love of the sea, using one finger in wet sand. Take a deep breath before entering this water…

All Summer Long

A CORNISH BEACH BOY

Kenny Maule

The Book Guild Ltd

First published in Great Britain in 2022 by
The Book Guild Ltd
Unit E2, Airfield Business Park
Harrison Road
Market Harborough
Leicestershire, LE16 7UL
Freephone: 0800 999 2982
www.bookguild.co.uk
Email: info@bookguild.co.uk
Twitter: @bookguild

A few names of characters have been changed to avoid identification

Typeset in 11pt Minion Pro
Printed on FSC accredited paper
Printed and bound in Great Britain by 4edge Limited

ISBN 978 1914471 049

British Library Cataloguing in Publication Data.
A catalogue record for this book is available from the British Library.

To Zoë my beloved mother who, assailed by life's storms and buffeted by personal misfortune, still cast her far-reaching lighthouse beams to guide her four world-faring children on the swirling currents of our planet.

Preface

This is not the full story, nor even full, nor even a story but a selective and unreliable account from a memory recorded unsteadily and now splurged selfishly on to the page.

Did you ever wish your youth could have been four years on a sand dune? Then read on, my sandy friend.

It has been aired that every first book should be autobiographical, and topics suggested to me were the early years of Cornish surfing, lifeguarding, flying training, supplying the North Sea build-up, instructing pilots in China and India during their airline 'explosion'.

Friends often suggested: "Why don't you write this damned book, then?" and I would reply: "Because a book needs structure and a *raison de composer*. Mine would be just a series of loosely unconnected anecdotes." Now, having run out of excuses, here goes, folks, in incriminating detail… on the crest of a wave, your future beckons.

1

Droppin' In...

The 'orses stood still, the wheels went aroun',
Goin' up Camborne hill, comin' down.
'CAMBORNE HILL' (TRAD. CORNISH FOLK SONG).

My motorbike's engine spread warmth on my Levi-ed legs as I slowed down, just short of Land's End, at the top of Sennen Hill, in the most westerly parish of Britain. I stopped, the sun now warming my helmet and the dribbling engine oil smelling sweetly, my surfboard bungee-ed to the side. The bike had given me a relieved, untroubled ride on the sharp corners and granite rises from St Ives through Eagles Nest, Gurnard's Head and Pendeen, although it's tricky to negotiate twenty miles of winding Cornish lanes when your surfboard, strapped alongside, allows only partial left-hand turns. Eagles Nest had frightened me when I bicycled this route as a thirteen-year-old. It was the reputed lair of the Wickedest Man in the World, Aleister Crowley, famous a few decades before. His 'nest' was a slated, gabled building straight from Alfred Hitchcock's set designer, sitting on a boulder-strewn peak, surrounded by scraggy trees, the home of rooks and ravens with all the pitch-black corvids swooping around small, but daring, cyclists. Past Tremedda Farm where I'd played in the barn with school pals, round by Gurnard's Head, the home of my oft-visited school pal, Malcolm, whose dad was the Coastguard. Pendeen was the site of old mining engine houses and chimneys, home of reputed tough kids that we beat at school football and rugby but from whom we had to flee before the referee packed up. Best be careful passing Pendeen, you might annoy the 'Knockers', reputed sprites who inhabit the dark regions below ground. Take care in Cornwall.

There were no observed rules in Pendeen apart from Methodism on Sundays and paganism on all other days. The place names around here are very Cornish, describing the landscape, 'By Tre, Pol and Pen shall ye know the Cornishmen'. Some say there's a fourth to be added, 'Ros', but then it doesn't scan, so it's 'Tre, Pol and Pen' (settlement, pool, and headland).

Looking down from on high, I could view the whole of Whitesand Bay, from near Land's End almost to Cape Cornwall. Afeart to descend its one-in-six hill – road surface crumbling a little, with an 'S' sign showing 'slippery' – my brakes were needing to cool so best to be in the lowest gear, braking with the engine. Get ye down that hill, boy; don't wish to be late for the start of a new life.

Before descending, I have a scan downwards onto my new domain. Am I reckless to lifeguard this beach on my own? At St Ives's Porthmeor Beach, we'd been six or seven manning a smaller, less-peopled surf beach. Now, here at Sennen's Whitesand Bay, I'd be on duty alone, with bigger surf, rippier rip currents and a much greater stretch of sand, both tide in and tide out. Whitesand Bay is well-named and renowned for big surf, with undulating

First steep descent to a life of wonder in Sennen on Whitesands Bay

hillocks of sand washed by swirling currents in their deep surrounds, a tidal range of six metres, about twenty feet.

Surf can only leave a beach in three ways: as undertow, as rip currents leading out to sea or as a combination of both. Sennen has everything at all stages of the tide and these factors change every day with the shifting sand, plus its big tidal range. I had explained all this three weeks ago at the council offices to an earnest interviewer. Of course, he didn't understand the complexities of Britain's beaches – very few do, even sailors – however, his job was to ensure he appointed someone who had some experience (me); seemed responsible (me); was first aid trained (me); very fit (me); and wished to be stuck in a wooden hut on its perch of a sand dune, without electricity or toilet or running water (happily me); oh, and undaunted by hundreds of potential drowners who flock to a beautiful beach near Land's End in the 'westiest' bit of West Penwith in West Cornwall in the West of England in Western Europe. The offer of 'go west, young man' I accepted willingly in return for a council wage for three summer months and the even closer attentions of girls my age (these were not guaranteed, but privacy was assuredly implied in the council's contract: 'We expect to visit you only once a fortnight, or less, and shall phone in advance'.

I still had fifteen minutes until my induction meeting outside Mrs Clifton's café below, so I surveyed the whole bay from the cliffs, dropping to Sennen Cove's tiny fishing harbour with its round winching shed and its steep, wooden, lifeboat slipway, past the lower car park and café, along the one-mile golden Whitesand Beach to intervening rocks, then Gwynver beach. Gwynver (Gwenver or Gwenvyr) was our sister beach, smaller but with bigger surf, too difficult for casual 'vacanciers' to descend its rocky, grassy cliff, just surfers, basking sharks, seals and occasional nudists, who were usually the girlfriends of the surfers, so 'watch out, mate!' Nudism, I preferred it not; if you happen to glance at someone, they assume you're ogling and don't appreciate remarks like, 'No, I'm not ogling, your homeliness discourages ogling'. The only attractive girls were friends of surfer pals, so also 'no ogling'.

In Gwynver Bay, grey seals would approach, hoping your surfboard was a fishing boat. Sitting splendidly alone on your board, a heavy breathing sound right behind can cause a sudden worry, especially as the seals often dive before you can be sure it actually was a seal, leaving behind only a suspicious splash. Scanning around, you then spot several basking sharks patrolling the bay – 'no teeth, but they can give you a nasty suck' you recite to yourself to buck your confidence. 'But what if today it's not a basking shark?' you nervously reconsider.

My binocs scanned the beach, then ranged on to more rocks, until the cliffs stretched away towards Cape Cornwall, with its remnants of tin-mine engine houses. Cape Cornwall was from the Cornish *Kilgoodh Ust*, meaning 'goose back of St Just' and was, until the first Ordnance Survey two hundred years ago, believed to be the most westerly mainland point in Cornwall. Nowadays, Land's End proudly holds that title and beams down upon the scenic Scilly Isles.

Oops, fifteen minutes of reflection gone, a quick, reassuring hoist of my sagging sleeping bag, kit and surfboard, and my BSA C15 squeaks its brakes down the one-in-six hill in cautious first gear.

Hmm, where's that council man? As agreed, we would meet at the café, just opening its shutters to welcome a slanting late-June sun peeking from behind the cliffs. Mysteriously, the staff all looked as though they were from the same family, because in fact they were: motherly Mrs Clifton, whom I came to love for her generous, free supply of yesterday's pasties and cakes to keep me alive for four summers; Mr Clifton, quiet but humorous; their beautiful daughter, who would marry my close and lucky school friend; and Derek, their son, who employed me on small building projects, keeping me in vital supplies of beer and petrol. Derek was almost mute, by choice, not by condition. I would come to know him well as we buried dead seals, built sea walls, caught fish, and discussed matters of random thought, he on practical matters, me on the broad romance of a life expected to be well-lived. Derek would never leave this small village cove; however, I would travel to almost every country on Earth. Derek, wily and money-wise, communicated only by sucking his teeth, the tones of which indicated his thoughts. Like with the complex tones of Cantonese, a tuned ear could generally discern his instructions.

"Shall I dig the hole over here, Derek?"

A short suck, "Soo-oo-ooh," with a rising tone = "Yes."

A long, flat suck, "Soo-oo-ooh," with a falling tone = "No."

A very short, sharp suck, "Soo-oo-ooh," = "Risky, wouldn't do that, boy!"

An imperceptible head nod indicates the desired digging spot. Tricky: you might think that nods of the head would prove difficult if he's calling you on the phone, but brief silences also indicated his thoughts. All who worked casually for Derek managed to understand him after a few learning errors. The spaces between teeth sucks also needed interpretation. These quirks are more easily understood in a small village with only one pub, its name The Old Success suggesting that everything would work out fine after a few pints. Serendipity rules if you relax enough to allow her an opportunity.

Sitting with a pot of tea, a digestive biscuit and a careful receipt, was my council manager, appointed to conduct my introduction to the lifeguard job. He remembered me from two months ago: "A bushy, bushy, blond hairdo... surfin' USA," and he decided I had come off this early production line of the factory of Cornish lifeguards (he puzzled, *how are they so tanned so very early in the season? Another of life's mysteries concerning these young bucks*). A brief handshake, a general chat, the introduction was a very small part of a manager's day and his office beckoned.

"Where shall we sit?"

"I'll sit here and you there," I said authoritatively. He looked askance at my cockiness. "Just so's I'll be facing the sea. It's now ten o'clock so I'm on duty already," I explained.

He peered doubtfully at the long, wide, empty beach, one girl walking two dogs: a golden retriever and a black lab. I would later discover she was Sandy, a fortuitously accurate name, as she had sandy hair and a freckly, sandy complexion; she was one of the few girl surfers and a general sand-lover, a pal of my sister as I'd discover later when it was almost too late. Knowing that a girl is a friend of one's sister can seriously disrupt desire, and so it would turn out. Also, sleeping with a surfer girl would seem almost like incest (and what could we talk about apart from surfing?). Anyway, I'd be surrounded by ex and current girlfriends. West Penwith was small and had too many girls, home-grown and visitors.

Mr Office brought me back to consciousness. "Our paperwork appears to be incomplete; I'll just fill in the details again." I suspected this to be a trick to check that I hadn't invented my original answers, given two months ago:

Date of birth:	22nd June 1951
School:	Humphry Davy Grammar, Penzance
Referees:	The Galloping Major, who set up St Ives Surf Club and John Payne, Council Manager
Religion:	Nominally Church of Scotland

With a start at this unexpected answer, he queried, "Does this mean you won't work on Sundays?"

My Lifeguard hut, atop the dunes. Friendly local, Sandy, greeting me warmly, 1969

I smiled tolerantly, reminding myself that Cornwall was Methodist and Wesleyan. "No, that's the Wee Frees named from the Free Church of Scotland. They're only free in the sense of rejecting the other churches; they're still enslaved to the same god. A self-invented belief system, like most."

"That's not very respectful."

"I do respect persons but not their group beliefs; after all, they vehemently don't accept mine. I'm an irredeemable sinner in their eyes."

"How do you know that?"

"Because, according to the Wee Frees, everyone is a sinner by definition, and they'll tell you to your face. Of course, I reckon they're as miserable as sin. Miserable, literally and metaphorically, not so much 'fishers of men' as 'drowners of optimism.'"

"What is your belief system then, if I may enquire, young man?" He barely suppressed his trowelled sarcasm.

"Moderate anarchist and cheerful pessimist."

Mrs Clifton brought more tea. Mr Office realised that, although enjoying the chat, he was, after all, paying for it whilst sitting in the sun. He asked for another receipt; working for the council was a secure job but not good enough to mean paying for one's own tea.

"May I put atheist?"

"No, because they're currently bottom of the religion list. I wish to be at absolute bottom, below even atheists. Most religions put themselves top, e.g, Muslim, Jew, Catholic, C of E… agnostic, atheist. Even Observant Cannibal is in there somewhere. It implies that they have carefully weighed the relative merits of unverifiable aspects. I wish to be uncategorisable in relation to their ideas, so cheerful pessimist it is."

"A-levels? Probably no results till August."

"Yes, actually, so far one A-level in Pure Maths with three others to come in August: Maths, Further Maths and Physics."

"That's an infinite amount of maths, isn't it?" he joked.

"Yes, it means I've never had to write an essay."

"So, you don't believe in essays? What's wrong with essays?" He defended his preferences.

"Well, essays are usually a way of outlining two sides of an argument, appearing to consider both carefully and then dispassionately coming to your original, hidden result, presenting it as a triumph of independence of thought. It's how politicians present themselves confidently as being possessors of all the answers. See 'religion' above," I said, spouting my own prejudices.

"Were you as combative at school?" he queried.

"Yes, and I'll kill the first person who says I wasn't."

He momentarily considered this, mentally filing it in the youthful humour category and sped on. "Would it upset you to know there is only one day off per week?" His pencil was poised.

"No upset to me, quite happy with that, it's already in the contract," I burbled cheerfully.

He scribbled something unseen, probably 'as daft as the others'. He outlined my duties as before:

lookout from 10am until 6pm (6pm luckily being the opening time of the Old Success, Sennen's quaint seventeenth century smuggling inn), managing the safe-swimming area with flags, keeping surfers out of the area, lost children, first aid, "Oh, and rescues too, if that's not too inconvenient, ha, ha."

And tools: orange float with rope attached, poles with flags, hi-vis jerkin, red-and-yellow canvas shorts, megaphone, fixed telephone, first aid kit, stretcher (my bed-to-be), binoculars and a logbook to record date/time of weather, surf, number on beach, rescues and results (!), casualties, dead seals and lost kids.

A third pot of tea beckoned – Mr Office was enjoying this: sun, affable chat, a bottomless pot of tea… but leaping suddenly to his feet, he announced, "To work!" and bounded towards the sand.

The sand, already hot; Mr Office in his black, overshined shoes sinking along; myself assured in bare feet, we set off walking in deep, dry sand, slowing as he tired. He gauged the distance to go, about eight hundred yards, should he take his shoes off and lose his status or keep them and lose his shine? He kept his status as barefootedness would be tantamount to 'going native'. We continued walking; this was now becoming my territory, home turf or home-marram grass, at least. Sand is a metaphor for different types of people: dry, warm, friendly or damp, resistant, hard-packed, or worst of all, wet, sinking, deadly. Already, the beach was reminding me of a beautiful girl; the higher sand is flaxen-coloured, the dunes swelling, enticingly rounded, grass billowing in the wind. Scattered along the sand, sheltering between sparkly, granite rocks, were a few early season beachgoers welcoming this cool-but-pleasant late-June day.

I liked him and he, too, me, but he seemed mystified at the chosen lifestyle of lifeguards. Why would anyone do this job, three months of the year, on a sometimes cold, lonely, windswept beach when a warm, comfortable office job with tea-making facilities was possibly available for a promising, young, grammar-school boy? He decided he'd never understand and, after checking my hut and contents, we parted. He turned as he left and mentioned with obvious distaste, "Yes, there's a little extra to be made if you choose to clean the beach, say before or after work, that would be paid 'off the books', quite generously, as we have no council cleaners who come out this way." Unaware of the daily shards of glass and well-filled nappies I would encounter, I beamed my grateful acceptance. The poet's 'bounty of the seas' is nothing compared to the actual bounty of a council-paid job, free hut, nearby pub, surfing when off duty and beach-cleaning off the books, followed by an end-of-season tax rebate. We shook hands and he re-scuffed his shoes on his return trudge, the familiar culture of his comfortable office awaiting him.

I glanced at the surf, no one in the water yet, early season.

Oh, the rolling of the sea is beckonin' to me…
NEWFOUNDLAND FOLK SONG FROM IRISH MUSIC,
ORIGINS OBSCURE.

2

Early Summer 1969

A Stout, Wee Hut...

There comes a tide in the affairs of men.
Which, taken at the flood, leads on to fortune;
Omitted, all the voyage of their life,
Is bound in shallows and in miseries.
On such a full sea are we now afloat...
BRUTUS, *JULIUS CAESAR.*

Mr Office leaves, and I, dressed in my canvas baggies and council jerkin announcing 'Lifeguard' to an indifferent world, sit atop the red box of my life-saving line, warm in the sun. I look from left to right, taking in the distant, tiny Sennen Cove harbour, protected partly by the Stones – a reef of jumbled, sharp rocks – with the Cove's appropriately tiny fishing fleet and round winching shed. How do you get small boats quickly from the surge of the harbour and up for protection on the hardstanding? You make a capstan and, over it, erect its winching shed – made from a low wall of crude, granite blocks – add a wooden structure and slate roof over a winding mechanism powered by men or donkeys, and 'heave away, haul away'. The boat slides up the beach and gravel onto the hardstanding until needed again.

That was Sennen Cove, supposedly named for Synt Senan, from whom comes the name of the River Shannon. History stalks you here.

Sennen Lifeboat, wooden slipway, 1969

The Royal National Lifeboat Institution (RNLI) shed stood well above, and to the right of the small harbour, with a wooden launch slide angled at forty degrees, a crewman would shout, "Shackles away, Shamuel!" The lifeboat would accelerate down the slide, hit the sea with an impressive ker-skoosh of water, bob to the surface and motor off to danger and adventure. RNLI crew: "We voluntarily risk ourselves for blithering fools whose lives are at risk through poor seamanship, bad judgement, recklessness, drunkenness, weather or mechanical failure." I paraphrase, for their traditional, respectful motto actually is, 'With courage, nothing is impossible', however the RNLI's history demonstrates that many things in reality are impossible, despite their well-documented heroism.

> *Sound off, the ships and all saluting, stand,*
> *Who sail in safety past the end of land –*
> *Land's End, where sea begins to do its worst –*
> *Last land for us, for foreigners the first,*
> *Here the brave sons of Sennen, volunteers,*
> *Have succoured seamen for a hundred years.*
>
> SIR ALAN HERBERT.

I put down my binocs and saw the pony-tailed girl, spotted earlier, walking with vim and vigour, free as a wheeling seagull, with her dogs lolloping around. Now, she was close enough, so I dropped down my sand dune. "Hello, I'm the lifeguard here, just arrived."

"Oh, 'ello." Slight accent, warm and friendly. I turned to walk with her. "You'll like round 'ere," she said confidently.

"Why?"

"Cos everyone does, that's why. Or they goes away again, but they'se makin' a big mistake, see."

"If they mistakenly go away, then I'm sure they'll return," I volunteered.

"Yes, but all at the same time again, they return – tha's the problem 'ere. You'll see, empty, then full for three months, then empty again for nine. Don't that bother ee? No work for nine months?" she warned me.

"Oh, three months here and nine at uni, I'll be like a migratory bird."

"There aren't any migratory birds round 'ere because they'd all be gone, wouldn't they?"

I wasn't sure whether that was a joke; perhaps West Penwith had a special humour. "What about you – do you migrate?" I ventured.

"Not usually, I'm not a bird, see."

Was that another joke? Hmm, not sure, I'll have to pay more attention. I ventured my own second-hand joke: "Them's nice birds."

"To you, all birds might look the same, but these're gulls," she said flatly.

"Well, gulls or boys, them's still nice birds. Dah, daaah!" Spike Milligan metaphorically turned in his grave. Metaphorically, because at this point, he was still alive.

A man of about forty ran past with a surfboard. Unusual, as most surfers were young; surfing was in its infancy in Britain. Intrigued, I turned to look after him.

"Tha's Mr Summerbee – ee's an 'elicopter pilot, P'zance to Scilly, 'as two boys, Kevin and Mike, good swimmers and runners both, got nice dogs, too. Every year, those boys wins the annual swim: The Brisons to Priest's Cove." Later, I discovered Sandy could turn this Cornish accent on and off for effect. Cornish for mystery or deeper knowledge, leaving others with a quizzical expression, then a normal accent for matters-of-fact.

I knew the Brisons to Priest's Cove swim was a short gap of dangerous waters, tidal flows, currents, full Atlantic swells and augmented by tricky chop and sucking wash, best avoided. Priest's Cove is an intimate cove, snuggled just west of St Just. The name is from the Cornish *Porth Ust*, the port or cove of St Just, truncated to *Por' Ust*, followed by a spelling error bringing Priest's Cove. Not all name origins can be solved so easily around here. The Brisons themselves, from the French *briser*, 'to break', are two jagged rocks sitting atop vicious reefs, wave-swept and unwelcoming, their intimidating rocks threatening boat and body. I was impressed that Kevin and Mike swam and won the annual race. They both went to my school, Kevin the better runner and Mike the better swimmer; a couple of years later, Mike would become my assistant when visitor numbers continued to increase. In those days, wetsuits were rare and expensive, most surfers making their own by gluing, stitching and taping neoprene rubber, then adding talcum powder before donning. Occasionally, city-dwelling swimmers, champions in indoor pools, would hear about the Brisons Race and enter, brimming with the confidence engendered by their warm, wave-free, indoor swimming lanes, their breathing regular and practiced. The reality of cold water here, currents dragging them off course and the chop disrupting their breathing, would soon bring them the embarrassment of being hauled out by the local fishing smack masquerading as a safety boat.

"Get an 'ot pasty inside o' ye, boy."

"A-a-r-re y-y-you the l-l-lifeboat?" The swimmers shiver.

"No, we'ez fishers of men, as the good Lord instructed us, see. Now get that 'ot pasty inside o' ye."

I turned to Sandy. "Are there any shops in Sennen or do I have to go the ten miles to Penzance?"

"Fish 'n' chips and a small grocers, otherwise it's P'zance. And you'll 'ave trouble getting your bike back up Sennen 'ill, 'specially with a girl on the back," Sandy warned and advised, "Go back along the sea road to take a run at it, careful in case a car turns across into the car park; change down sooner than later; keep the revs up."

Had she guessed I had a motorbike? Did she have a motorbike? Had she already inspected my bike and spotted the worn sprockets? Was that 'girl on the back' an assumption? I didn't know Sandy. Was she volunteering as a pillion passenger? Did she know me? We had now reached the car park. She turned to follow her dogs.

"Do you know me?" I asked askance.

"You're from Porthmeor Beach in St Ives, like the Williams boys, Charles, James and the other one and their sister."

"You have an advantage over me," I stated regally. "But, anyway, thank you for talking to me, an imperfect stranger." Regally, again.

"Imperfect, I'm sure you are, but I think I already knows ee pretty well, see." She turned to follow her Labradors. "You're Kenny Maule, tidn't like you're anyone special, see."

Feeling somewhat that I'd lost a conversation that was not actually a competition, I stumped happily up my sand dune. Time to peruse my disappointing furniture. A hard-canvas stretcher and a thin, single mattress, one chair (wobbly), one small gas burner. Washing had to be with minimal water or I'd have to frequently visit the public toilets for a top-up from the rear tap, or into the sea first for soaping, especially if it was conveniently raining, then I could quickly rinse myself coming ashore, and mount my sand dune to warm up.

I hung up my damp, home-made wetsuit. In those days, we made our own suits, the recipe being: buy not-quite-enough sheet-neoprene, girlfriend outlines your shape in paper, cut, check it fits, cut neoprene generously then trim, glue together, check again, stitch with stout thread, and glue tape over the seams. Freezing early-season water will pass impartial judgement.

My stout, wee hut, proudly atop its dune-top eyrie, comprised a half-concrete floor, probably a leftover WWII lookout-cum-machine-gun nest,

Alert, vigilant, sober and always on guard

and half-wood walls with the top half of the front boasting a commanding panorama of the whole beach through a wide glass and plastic pane. The view was down sun from dawn until afternoon, a glare-free sight of the beach and bay from Land's End all the way to Cape Cornwall's headland. With binocs, the bathers were in clear sight and the passing shipping rounded Land's End for my personal entertainment. From the slope above, the Scilly Isles smudged the horizon twenty-five miles to the west. In a night's bad weather, my hut resembled an Aussie tin-roof Queenslander. The hut would reverberate to the noisy drum of torrential rain and screaming wind but in my memory, the morning would always give me dry sand, shimmering with rising heat and a welcoming warmth radiating from the glass-wood front. You would generally expect old wartime lookouts to be on the cliff tops but not so. Like the Cape of Good Hope's two lighthouses, Cornwall's cliffs often are wrapped in cloud and drizzle, so lower lookouts have the advantage. The coming de-manning of the lighthouses had piqued my interest, so I already knew that at the Cape of Good Hope they had even built a second, lower lighthouse *below* the first, as the frequent low cloud had too often obscured the upper. It's not always sunny in the south, maties.

In centuries gone by, flotillas of Spanish ships would sporadically invade West Cornwall, knowing that the king's men were two days' ride away, then some frantic mustering was required, followed by two days' return ride. By this time, the Spanish invaders had been safe for five days and plundered unbothered into undefended villages. A few kidnapped local squires could be ransomed for a bag of silver, but with a population of poor farmer fishers, of accumulated wealth was there little, perhaps a smattering of silver goblets, however of cattle and women was there plenty, and plenty was taken. Women were violated and likely youngsters were taken for the white slave trade in North Africa. In return, the Spanish 'taking and giving' is still evidenced today in the population, seen in the many people who are smaller with dark hair and dark eyes. Several hundred years later, this would result in my own good fortune, as my girlfriend-to-be attracted my roving eye at a party. Her family were all fair, but she was definitely a reversion to Spain: olive skin, ebony-black hair and dark eyes. I spotted her from across the room but strangely, no one was chatting her up, her beauty intimidating the lads. Unusually, I too was shy, so I asked her friend to ask her whether I had her permission to ask her out. Roundabout but successful. Her beauty radiated like the rotating flashes of a lighthouse, blinding all comers. Her face was often serene, then she would turn and smile, dazzlingly hypnotic.

Sometimes, wind-driven, Spanish galleons would anchor off Whitesand Bay, for no Spanish ship could risk coming closer than one mile to this surf-shrouded beach. The galleons would lower their boats and loot at will. One incident entered the local legends. As the Spanish raiders advanced over the dunes, a local lad had been gathering seaweed and was caught unawares. He started up the hill just behind my hut, sack on his back, arrows zipping into his sack. Terror-motivated, he made it to the top and, once up, he alerted one and all to ready their ploughshares, staffs and staves. This was seldom a successful defence and managed retreats were hampered by the farmers driving their only wealth, their cattle.

West Cornwall has farms atop her high, unscalable cliffs, but the view from above the coastline allowed, from time long past, to continually monitor the herring shoals passing Land's End. Herring meant bounty and manna, but fishing offshore from a boat required a rarely gentle sea. The good Lord, however, had sent sustenance for the faithful followers of Methodism and John Wesley. As the shoals meandered, feeling their way, the villagers prayed the fish would enter the bay. Once they entered, the trap was set. Womenfolk gathered baskets and barrels. Menfolk would row across the bay, looping their nets, shrouding the fish, driving them shorewards. With the shoals trapped, the sea would boil with frantic fish – closer, closer, tighter, denser – then the women and children, grannies and grandads, would plunge into the surf, pulling the nets in, scooping like billy-o, the fish flapping onto the sands, everyone working with a frenzy now; common sharing would come later.

'Onan hag Oll' – Cornwall's motto: 'One and All'.

Anyway, time to unpack. Surfboard outside, protected in the hut's shade, I must remember to bring it in at night, you never knew when a passing Cornish wrecker might happen upon a bounty. Short and triple-finned, my board was not efficient to catch waves, so you had to take off at the steepest moment of the wave, just before it broke; it was quick to turn though, not like the long malibu boards we'd started on as kids in St Ives. In the early '60s, only the main beaches had lifeguards: Newquay, St Ives. The lifeguards were mainly Aussies, rough drinkers who delighted in foul-mouthed utterings sprinkled with Aussie slang. They played up to this idea of the bronzed, grizzled, Aussie boozers who treated girls badly and were hungover until midday; that's midday on the overmorrow! By comparison, we locals were good-natured, mainly grammar-school kids who could swim well, sporty and had joined the Galloping Major's Surf Life-Saving Club. The Galloping Major had spent time abroad, where he'd seen surfing, and his teenagers were both good surfers. The Major saw the Club as a watery version of clean youth. He'd charmed and bullied the local St Ives Council into supplying premises, perfectly overlooking Porthmeor Beach, and the 'clean youth' took over the lifeguarding at the weekends so the Aussies could pursue their natural proclivities for two sleepless days and nights. We ran up and down, getting even fitter, practising with reels and ropes, swimming out and being pulled in, looking for lost children. On wet days, we could easily monitor the few holidaymakers, locally known as grockles, while we took it in turns to surf, do minor first aid, listen to the radio comedies and play cards. Cards were weirdly my chance. I'd come in with a rugby pal, Alastair, who wanted me to join and decided to introduce me, a full five years younger than these men of eighteen to twenty years. I'd explained to Alastair that I was broke so couldn't join the Club. As the heavy rain drove the grockles off the beach, he advised me to start making friends by playing cards and lent me a small stake. Pontoon, this I could play a bit, and with a string of lucky hands, I realised I had just enough for club membership. I victoriously stacked my cards, scooped up the cash and paid my fee using their money, surrounded by howls of 'unfair, dude'. Luckily, I knew them all from school rugby teams, so I got away with it, just. Now a proud member, I offered to buy everyone a beer when I next fell into money and nervously fled into the rain. Thus, a surfer I became. If you're going to misspend your youth, then do it to glorious advantage.

There was, of course, the small matter of learning to surf without a surfboard and currently no surf, but Lady Luck would provide if sufficient effort were added to the mix.

"I urgently need a surfboard." I rushed in to inform my mother.

"Why would you urgently need a surfboard?"

"Because I've already joined the Surf-Life-Saving Club and it cost me £10. Every day I don't have a surfboard will progressively devalue my £10."

"But when you left this morning, you didn't have any money at all."

"Ah, via pontoon, I've now joined the club and I still don't have any money and so effectively I have even less without a surfboard."

This conversation ended with my stepfather-to-be's drunken entrance, slurring his seafaring speech with well-practised, outdated slurs: "On my crew, lazy buggers like you'd be clapped in irons."

"Buggers seem to feature greatly in your crew, sailor," I risked to reply, edging away.

"Get out of here before you're lashed to a pulp." He raised his hand and lurched forwards.

I stepped outside and into my new life: money was the key and speed was the lubrication. Hitch-hiking the five miles back into St Ives led to a chance conversation that led to a suggestion that led to me applying for a café job on Porthmeor Beach. The café was run by a fearsome, elderly lady called Peggy, my colleagues informed me sniggeringly. At that point, the door opened and in limped Peggy. I ignored her wooden leg, failing to make the obvious 'peg leg' connection and announced: "Hello, Peggy, pleased to meet you; my name is Kenny." The others sniggered even more uncontrollably behind me.

"Hello, Kenny, my name is *not* Peggy." As she limped past, I realised with horror that I'd been had. Grey as a bloodless greyhound on an overcast wintery day, I started to apologise, but she cut me short. "My name is Meg, sometimes Meggy, and I pay those who work hard."

"Ah, yes, my mother used to have a café here and working hard for her was my great joy. It was called the Sugar n' Spice, maybe you remember it?" I bumbled on cheerily.

"Yes, I know your mother; she had a reputation as a social butterfly and she ran the greatest café in the world. You start tomorrow at nine o'clock. And by the way, I'm not your mother; I'm your boss. Cleanliness here is not next to godliness; it's grubbiness that's next to sackingness."

That was clear for me, and I was in heaven. I could surf before work, surf at lunchtimes, and surf after work, with free pasties (three days old) and the gloried status of being part-time employed. These were times in the '60s when cafés had sticky buns and three-day-old pasties. On day four, standing on the café balcony, we chucked them to the seagulls, whose squadrons darkened the sky. We were supposed to break up the pasties but that was pandering to the gulls, so I often chucked up larger and larger pieces, intrigued to discover the maximum load a gull could catch and hold as gravity screamed it downwards. They faced the choice of following the piece into the sand or dropping it and pulling out of a high-G death dive. The feathers on the upper wing would rise as the gull increased its aerodynamic load. Hmmm, aerodynamics, maybe that would interest me later.

True to my word, I bought my new surfing pals a beer from my next Friday's pay. I was suddenly rich beyond compare, with two part-time jobs, the café and deckchair hire with my deckchair 'boss' Bruce. Bruce paid with my money as I humbly stood outside the pub and the older surfers drank within. That was expensive, a week's pay, but I'd firmly established my surfing 'dudeness' status: I could play cards, keep my word, surf a bit, and I understood the importance of beer. Almost a full dude. Next summer, I'd join them in the pub as I'd reach the almost-legal drinking age of fifteen (which in St Ives was OK if one were as tall as an eighteen-year-old). Take care to wear motorcycle boots to be taller, not flip-flops – they're for real adults.

Enough reflections on the vagaries of life. Would I be lonely here in my solitary lifeguard hut, no TV or radio, just yesterday's newspapers salvaged from the beach and the library books I'd ferried on my bike? I'd already often been alone as we'd moved house in Scotland a couple of times and then down to Cornwall, all before I was age ten. I'd spent my solitary, friendless times walking the many beaches near St Ives, jumping rocks along the coast, teaching myself to swim confidently, even managing to save a younger lad on Porthminster Beach, much to the relief of his shrieking mother. He had slipped from the old diving board off the rocks. This board had many dangers. The water was absent at low tide, just dry sand, but was adequately diving deep at high tide, as it happened to be that day. My life-saving skills were not yet existent, but I jumped in. He clung to my neck, so I had to swim breaststroke, unable to take a proper breath. We inched our way to the beach, avoiding the wave-bashed rocks beyond the diving board. Funnily enough, that would be the only time I was ever thanked for a rescue. The mother shepherded her wayward son up the beach, alternately kissing him, hugging him, scolding him, and slapping him round his flanks. Still gasping for breath, I was unable to thank her for thanking me, but her appreciations had made an impact on this adolescent boy as I trudged home, my mother noting my dripping clothes as I unthinkingly made my way upstairs. I was child number four; she had already seen everything and I was safe in the knowledge that my big brother Eoin had already committed more sins in his twenty years than I would in my whole existence. My chief advantages in life were a cheery, winning smile and naturally curly, blond hair, gaining confidence from much bosom-hugging by aunties, shopkeepers and neighbours. This confidence would take me far in an uptight world, as I would subsequently discover.

Coming from Ayrshire to Cornwall at the age of ten, I never felt lonely, but I was mainly alone, and I had six months in the St Ives Primary, making some temporary friends there. After the eleven-plus exam, I went straight to the grammar, leaving my new-found pals behind, quickly making new friends at the grammar, but we were soon put in different sets, so again I lost

Babe in arms, Ayrshire 1951, and happy schoolboy, Penzance 1963

them. As I'd moved schools in Scotland and Cornwall, I seemed destined to have only temporary friends, and my subsequent life as a pilot would follow the same pattern.

I played all the sports, and our school teams were, in the main, county champions. To play in the school teams meant a lad was immune to punishment for his sins. When dragged by a teacher to our headmaster, accused of mortal sins, I was usually let off by the headmaster excusing me. "This boy is in the Under 13s, 14s, 15s and will make the first team – I'll warrant," he would say to the enraged teacher.

The downside was my surname 'Maule' as I played loose-head flanker or tight-head prop, which allowed unoriginal teachers to make obvious jokes, such as, "You've got a loose head this morning, Maule, do you need propping up?" Admirable, three puns in one question, brimming with teacherly sarcasm.

My strong West of Scotland accent was also an endless source of jokes, but mainly my school mates were good-natured and for this, I still feel compelled to visit Cornwall often and defend it in all conversations, especially from those across the Tamar. I still say, "You might think the Cornish are a bit dim, but they're cannier than the Scots. You'll always have less money in your hand after you've met them and grateful for the experience."

How did I get into this professional lifeguarding game? My pal Mick, already nineteen and two years older than me, had recently suggested lifeguarding as he was planning to do the same at Porthcurno Beach and had already been approved by the council. On winter weekends we worked together endlessly on our bikes, his a Triumph Bonneville 500, mine a BSA C15, then a Velocette 350 single with fishtail silencer, then a 200cc Triumph Tiger Cub and soon to buy a Triumph 350. We played squash at the Cable and Wireless college where the transatlantic cables disappeared into the Atlantic depths, to emerge 2,500 miles later at Newfoundland. The Cable & Wireless college was remote down here, but it was stringing the Commonwealth together and variously connecting the whole world. The college had foreign students from everywhere, including the most exotic islands, and I discovered from my defeats that Pakistanis, Indians and Egyptians were the world's top squash players and for good reason.

After a few drinks in Penzance, Mick and I would speed up to the weekly midnight horror film at Camborne, girlfriends on our pillions, in the cloudy, cool summer nights, racing back along the A30, Cornwall's longest road, stretching from London, ending at Land's End. Our girlfriends had the greatest trust, riding behind two schoolboys, influenced by alcohol, in the dark, on dodgy bikes, with only six-volt headlights. As Elizabeth Barrett Browning questioned, "How do I love thee? Let me count the ways. Enough to ride pillion behind thee?"

With both of us council lifeguards, we needed one day off per week, usually the quietest days, and we could appoint 'suitable' friends to replace us, paying them casually from our 'floats'. Mick and I usually just exchanged beaches and paid each other, thus working seven days per week but adding handsomely to our grubby savings. I needed to support myself through the winters and Mick was already saving to emigrate to Australia, his well-kept secret. He wasn't academic, more practical, so Oz held more possibilities for him. I was more academic and would go to uni, but together we had squash, bikes, beaches, humour and gorgeous girlfriends in our foursome paradise.

Funnily, I never fancied Oz despite, or maybe because of, knowing enough Aussie lifeguards. They were few in number but large in life, guzzling alcohol, swearing, questionable personal habits and full of fighting talk. I was convinced that most of them were illiterate, but there was no way to know this for sure, and it would be dangerous to enquire. When summer surfing competitions were happening, they would compete, win, get drunk and sleep on the beach. One Friday night, the guy, fondly named 'The Animal from Oz', was chucked out of the Porthtowan Beach pub an hour before closing time for being more drunk than the regulars, that in itself being quite an achievement. He swore, threatened, and broke glass but stormed off into the night's sand dunes. We, only slightly ashamed for our 'Animal' friend, carried on drinking happily; anyway, he had a tendency to spoil evenings. After all were asleep in tents in the sand dunes, The Animal crept back into the pub, opened the till, crapped into the drawers, pushed down his 'efflux' and closed the till. He left the loose coinage in there for maximum effect, he told us later. At opening time, he was the first customer, smiling merrily as the barmaids cashed in and then passed out. When he later boasted of this, his already-waning popularity plummeted to Davy Jones's locker. A joke is one thing, but these actions weren't a joke and didn't smell too good. He was greatly offended when we didn't approve, and he accused us of being pompous Poms. The Animal was then aptly renamed 'The Arse from Down Under'. Time to replace these unmanageable Aussies with good, upstanding sons of Blighty, however first, we had to learn surfing from these wave-riding ogres; they knew how to surf, that was undeniable, and by comparison we were wannabe sprites of the waves but fast catching up.

I could not help concluding, that this man felt the most supreme pleasure, while he was driven on, so fast and so smoothly, by the sea.
CAPTAIN COOK ON FIRST ESPYING A HAWAIIAN SURFER.

3

Summer 1969

But Where Does the Water Go?

Consider the subtleness of the sea; how its most dreaded creatures glide under water, unapparent for the most part, and treacherously hidden beneath the loveliest tints of azure.

HERMAN MELVILLE, *MOBY DICK*.

First real day on the job, a few choppy waves with a light onshore wind, tide low and just about to turn, quite sunny. Did I expect a lot of tourists? Possibly. It was a very warm morning, and I could see over to the car park; it was starting to fill up; our resident Liverpudlian, communist car park attendant John was gesticulating to drivers and waving his arms. I hadn't met him yet, but I surely would; he was the nicest man possible: generous, humorous, bearded with a vocalised hatred of capitalism and leader of the People's Resistance Against Leaving Dogs in Hot Cars on Sunny Days. He was patiently explaining about car windows and water to a couple who didn't understand that the sun they desired would drive their dog crazy, at best, or kill it at worst. The first families were now stumbling towards the beach, arms filled with clobber; picnic hampers, baby-changing stuff, inflatable toys and bags of just, well, stuff. Why do they need so much? They survey the beach and decide on which positions they should begin arguing about. Pointing and waving their hands, our first family drop their clobber twice and start again. Husband has won the argument about their

22

chosen site, and they bumble towards it, like unshepherded refugees. Poor choice, they're heading down towards the tideline. I'm distracted by a small child with a cut knee, her parents complaining about glass on the beach, a perennial problem. By the time I'm finished, the first family has started setting up and the breadwinner husband is returning from the shop with windbreaks and deckchairs. They didn't waste any time; holidaymaking is a serious business and lots of 'stuff' is essential. I make my way down the beach with my megaphone; I'll need that soon with an incoming tide. Our first family is now well-ensconced two metres above low tide.

"Good morning, everyone, may I give you some advice?"

"If you want," says hubby suspiciously. "Like what?"

"Like you're just here at low tide and, in a few minutes, you'll have to move."

"Who says?"

"Well, not me personally, just the laws of physics; the tide is turning and starting to come in; you'll be wet in a few minutes."

"How's that then? There's no big waves."

Ah-ha, another British man who, despite being nearly forty years old and a citizen of a patriotically maritime nation, has failed to spot the difference between tides and waves. How will I explain this without humiliating him?

Luckily his wife butts in. "I told 'im about tides but he wouldn't listen. Now you tell 'im."

"OK, the tide will be coming in and you really need to move well up the beach."

He looks around at his clobber, irritated. "So 'ow far's it goin' to come, then?"

"Well, you see that line of seaweed way up there? That's 'ow far." Careful, careful, I remind myself, don't mimic people's accents; I might be just eighteen, but I know that they don't like it, especially if they sport tattoos. It used to be that tattoos indicated a sailor, but now it's city-dwellers and they never understand tides.

"'Ow do you know that then, mate? There's seaweed on a lot of your beach 'ere." Oh-oh, some aggression in the voice.

"Ee knows cos ee's the lifeguard, see, it's wrote on 'is jacket." This wife is helping my cause; I know how these conversations can go. She starts to pack up and grumbles, "I told 'im but ee don't listen to me. I told 'im further up the beach, anyways, it's closer to the ice-cream."

I thank them and move on with my megaphone. "Please, everyone, move further up the beach; the tide is coming in quickly; we have spring tides today. Further up the beach."

As I return, our first family's hubby is telling others, "Oh yeh, move yourselves, yes, up to the line of seaweed, they get big tides 'ere, don't wanna get caught out, do we." Phew. "Hey, mate," he calls, "what's your name, then?"

"Kenny, like Kenny Rogers." I always had to add the Rogers bit. Kenny is not a common name in England.

"Mine's George, like King George, pleased to meet you; anyway, they don't 'ave these 'ere tides in the Med, you know."

"Yes, you're right, but our six-metre tides clean our beaches nicely, twice a day, and leave piles of rotting seaweed for the farmers' potatoes."

"'Ear that, Dotty? Our tides is better than theirs," he opined patriotically. A friendly nod to George and Dotty and I pass on.

Holidaymakers come for a perfect time, but beaches are not without risk. There are common dangers – wasp stings, jellyfish, broken glass in the sand – however, there are also less-common risks. I'd recently become aware of weever fish, via an article in the local Cornishman newspaper. Further up the coast, several people and dogs had been stung. I needed to know soon where this fish hid, where it moved and how to combat it. Beachgoers can, and do, tread on weever fish just under the sand in Cornwall. In the 1970s it was not easy to find information if one lived near Land's End, but this was important; will the next victim be on Sennen Beach and will this lifeguard know what to do? If I wished to know some facts, then I had to visit Penzance library, find a reference book, remember the information or take notes and draw some supporting images. Very often, we relied on word-of-mouth, and that's like Chinese whispers. As I was always manning the beach at library opening times, I had to ask my girlfriend, who readily volunteered, and a mere two days later, I had the bare facts. Weevers! These small, sand-coloured fish bury themselves into the sand, and if you stand on them, their dorsal fin pierces your foot and injects the venom from spines on its back, carrying a neurotoxin that causes extreme, excruciating pain, which is variable according to temperature. In the first two hours, the pain is often described as agonising; the foot goes red and swells, then it will feel numb until the following day, with irritation and pain that may last for up to two weeks. It can even cause abdominal cramps, not good if you're in the sea! How to treat it? Immerse the affected area in water as hot as tolerable for an hour. Use tweezers to remove any spines. Scrub the wound with soap and water and then flush extensively with fresh water. Wounds to be left open.

Some weever fish were reported near Porthtowan and Newquay. I hoped they would stay there but two weeks later, guess what? One lady was walking in the shore surf, was stung and fell in waist-deep water. She floundered and was retrieved by her accompanying family. Much screeching followed, as expected, and after the recommended treatment, I sent her to hospital. I didn't ask whether the pain was worse than childbirth; judging by her cries, I reckoned it probably was.

Only surfers fully understand sets of waves. The sea can be calm, especially if the waves are from a distant storm, and then a set of waves comes in, generally seven in a row, the third usually being the biggest. There is the added complication of tides; the water goes rapidly further out and stays there for two hours – 'slack water' – hardly changing, then returns much faster, being fastest at mid-tide. On a shallow beach, it covers the sand quickly, softening it in advance so you cannot run, only squelch. The fortnightly spring tides are even greater and faster. Then, of course, there are rip currents due to surf water coming onto the beach. This surf is now piling up and must leave by rips or undertow. Rips move in deeper water as they scour a runnel. If being dragged out, one must relax by floating till the rip spreads and diminishes further offshore, then swim *across* the beach and come in where there is no rip, a difficult idea to master when you're exhausted, cold and becoming panicky. Surfers happily use all these effects to their advantage.

Great danger, a rip current takes you out, easy to spot from above.
Credit David Clark, Woods Hole Oceanographic Institution

A few days later, I see George and Dotty again. George, now wearing a Union Jack paper hat, is revelling in his new-found knowledge of tides and waves as he helpfully informs his fellow grockles about tidelines and seaweed. He saunters over. "'Ere, Kenny, so where does all this water go when the tide goes out? Someone arsked me 'bout that."

"Well, George, it depends on the shape of the coastline and the mass of the sea or ocean."

"Whaddya mean, like?"

"Well, on this Atlantic coast, the tide goes up the coast; each port is ten or fifteen minutes later as you go up. On smaller seas, like the North Sea, it tilts up on one side and down on the other, then switches. It's pretty complex."

"Som'un said the water piles up in the middle – is that stupid then?"

"No, that's true in some oceans. It's all to do with size, shape, depth, water mass and coastline shape."

"Oh, that's good; the wife don't know nothin' 'bout all this." He sped off to glory in his male knowledge.

I pass on to shift my swimming-area flags, and ten minutes later, George is at my side with two enormous Cornish ice-creams, decorated with 99s and topped-off with hundreds and thousands. "We're off tomorrow early; this is our last day; I can't buy you a pint so 'ere's the next best thing," and he thrust an overburdened cornet into my sandy hand.

"Nice to know you, George, and next year we can talk about water temperatures and this global warming; it's a new science; I'm planning to learn something over the winter."

George beamed and vigorously shook my sandy hand; my ice-cream wobbled.

"We're definitely comin' 'ere next year; you can bank on it."

I wandered off, waving to Dotty and the kids. I must learn something about this new greenhouse effect because it's now urgent as George'll quiz me; I've got only eleven months to prepare.

Changing after a post-work surf, I see Sandy's neighbour, Mr Summerbee, heading to the surf. His name was easy to remember as it was summer and he flew helicopters, the buzzing bees of the sky that passed over us en route to Scilly. He nodded and I intercepted him. "Hello, I understand you're Mr Summerbee, a helicopter pilot."

"Yes, and I've got exactly one hour in the surf, then I must go. Talk to you next time." In that brief interchange, I understood the precision, directness, intent and timing one needs to be a pilot.

Mr Summerbee didn't forget as, a few days later, while peering through my rain-glazed window at a wet, windy beach, he came over the back hill, knocked briefly and dropped into my hut, shaking his waterproofs, reckoning correctly that I wasn't busy as there were few rain-challenged grockles on the beach. "There's no good surf, so let's chat. Is that a gas burner for coffee? I'm on standby, so I may need to rush off." He pointed at his pager.

Unknown to me, this conversation would firm up my ideas and change my direction in life. I busied myself with the coffee as he looked around critically.

"Maxwell House coffee, Mr Summerbee?" I hoped he'd say 'yes' as I neither knew, nor had, any other coffee. The rain increased, so going to the café was not an option. I selfishly hoped the rain would blank his pager signals as this was my one chance to chat with a real pilot. There wasn't even a proper airport in Cornwall, only the military runway at Newquay and the heliport at Penzance, two flights daily to the Scilly Isles.

"So, you have ambitions to be a pilot?"

"Yes, definitely, but I know nothing about it yet."

"Don't worry about that; pilots are usually away-away-oh in other lands, so they have no time to give explanations. I can explain."

"So, how does one start?"

He settled in, trying to get comfy in my one wobbly chair. "That's a big problem, but you'll overcome it if you're good enough and focused on your goal. First, *why* do you want to fly? It's a difficult life at the beginning, then it gets better, for most of us that is. There's always some risk and just losing your medical can be the end." Another sip of coffee. "Aviation in itself is not inherently dangerous, but to an even greater degree than the sea, it is terribly unforgiving of any carelessness, incapacity or neglect," he recited carefully so that I would realise it was a well-known quote (well-known amongst pilots, anyway, who generally don't mention the word 'danger' to their passengers).

"That's a good quote, an aphorism even, as it's also true of lifeguarding and motorbiking," I added to show understanding.

He looked at me carefully, taking in my 'bushy, bushy' blond hair. "Are you on the arts or science side at school?"

"The science side, maths and physics mainly. With a bit of spare-time reading thrown in." I carelessly gesticulated towards my two books for rainy-day reading: *Catch 22* and *Moby Dick*. I was happy for the rain as sunny weather meant less reading and I'd soon be paying overdue library charges, more pleading required on my poor student theme.

I needed to show some interest. "Well, I've seen a few heli-rescues near St Ives and several on the cliffs around here and occasionally offshore. It's amazing to watch the winchman dropping down, dangling above a ship or the waves. Quite an adventure, looks even better through binocs."

"So, you'd fancy being a winchman then?"

"No, just the pilot, it looks like a good mix of skill and sufficient brains, being in charge of all that, especially as they seem to be busy in the most beautiful places, mountains, islands, coasts…"

"Yes, but chopper pilots are also in horrible places like Equatorial Africa and wherever there's oil activity. Mind you, that's also a major challenge, trying to avoid small wars, and you've no maintenance at times, all the crew sleeping in barracks in steamy jungles for months." Mr Summerbee checked his watch. "Well, I started in the Navy, on ships and air-sea rescue, medical flights, then the North Sea Oil build-up off Aberdeen, some stints in the steamy bits of Africa."

I interrupted pointlessly with, "Better to sleep with a sober cannibal than a drunk Christian."

He laughed, glanced pointedly at my library copy of *Moby Dick* and continued. "Then, I joined the British Airways helis and now I do the Penzance to Scilly run. That's truly beautiful, passing Mousehole, Land's End and then the islands. Often repetitive, but you can expect tricky weather at times. And in winter, we do stints in other, less-forgiving places. Still loving it after all these years."

The near-empty gas burner coughed again, and I served the coffee in my unsuitable cups, proffering a stained bag of coagulated sugar beside some dodgy, dehydrated milk. He wisely took it black with no sugar. "I'll bring you down some fresh milk tomorrow; there's some surf forecast, so I'll be down. Anyway, why does a well-read, young scientist like yourself plan to be a pilot?"

I answered with a smile, "Having little or no money in my purse, and nothing particular to interest me on shore, I thought I would—"

"OK, stop it with the *Moby Dick* quotes; my old memory is fading," he hooted.

I continued, "Seriously though, I have the advantage of knowing absolutely nothing about flying, so I have an uncluttered mind. I reckon only football, film direction and piloting afford a likely lad from Cornwall the three things necessary in life: sufficient money, comely girls and a challenge."

"So, that's it, these three things."

"I'm sure there's a lot more to flying, but I'm guessing you're going to tell me all that matters."

"OK, you're listening now?" he queried.

I smiled and nodded. "I'm all ears but no one's perfect." Was that one irritating joke too many?

He ignored that remark, looking at his watch again. "I've got thirty minutes to tell you the main points, so switch off your 'Transmit' and switch on your 'Receive', my boy."

The following thirty minutes told me everything I needed to know and convinced me I wanted to work with Mr Summerbee, yeah *Captain* Summerbee, as I would travel the world in search of money, romance and unforeseeable challenges.

Explanations finished, he stood up, handing me my unsuitable cup. "They sell good seconds at the pottery come end of season." Compact information with tact, I liked that.

He ducked out, waved a hand and ran straight up the hill from a standing start. *Hmmm*, I thought, *these pilots need to be fit, too.* Add that to the list. I reflected on his advice: Apply to the Navy, the Air Force and British Airways. Add aviation to other studies when at uni and join the university air squadron if you can. Captain Summerbee was right, but I carefully avoided his guidance, being a big-headed git. I'd come back to it after travelling extensively in the Americas; I'd use his name as a reference and then scrupulously follow his good advice to the tee.

At school, I'd told the career master that I wished to become a pilot, but he'd explained that was impossible as 'no boy from this school has ever become a pilot'. I responded that I didn't consider that an obstacle and immediately left the room.

Piloting is a mix of coordination, skills, technical knowhow, plus clear priorities under pressure. I desired exciting travel, good money and the company of beautiful girls. I had never flown. So, when I was almost too old at twenty-three and with absolutely no air experience or money, I would eventually defy the odds and manage to fly with the three best airlines in the entire world, a long story for next time.

For hours, I reflected on our conversation and the possibilities Captain

Summerbee had explained: would I be able to become a pilot? Waking from my reverie, I realised the surf had improved, the rain had stopped and I'd need to dash into the surf for an hour of pleasure before the sun finally set over Cape Cornwall.

Almost upon the western wave
Rested the broad, bright Sun.
SAMUEL TAYLOR COLERIDGE,
THE RIME OF THE ANCIENT MARINER.

After a few days, I received my first phone call, jumping with a sudden jerk. Who would call me here? Who would know I'm here, apart from girlfriend Mirren? So far, I'd just called out a few times ('use sparingly', advised the council). "Dringgg, dringgg," the phone rang again. I answered cautiously, expecting a request for a lost child search. "Hello, Sennen Lifeguard."

"Kenneth, it's your darling mother calling."

"Mother, how did you get my number?"

"Oh, we inveigled it from Fiona, so I decided to call and see how my youngest offspring is doing."

Now, I purposely had not given out my number to avoid the phone ringing on its loudspeaker whilst I was busy on the beach. I'd feared running across a beach and up a steep sand dune to discover a wrong number or a joke call from drunken pals. "How did my delightful sister Fiona get my... oh, forget it. What can I do for you, Mother Dearest?"

"Bungey and I are meeting some of Bungey's old shipmates at the Tinners Arms in Zennor next week and wish to hear your latest tales of derring-do and watery mishap."

Bungey was my stepfather, a retired sea captain, rough of tone and desirous of drink. He viewed me as a long-haired lout. "You'd never have served on my ships; my crew were real men, you young scallywag."

To counter his expansive criticisms, I'd take issue with his language to irritate him. "Define scallywag, my honourable captain, and long-haired implies hair, lank and greasy. Mine is curly, high not long, think Garfunkel. Lout, I'll allow you that word but only as a concession." These backchats raised his blood pressure; picture Captain Pugwash in a rage. I'd started staying away from home by the age of sixteen, after Bungey would challenge me to fights and then think better of it and just chuck me out. I ended up sleeping the summer nights in the deckchair hut on Porthgwidden Beach, where I held the grand position of assistant deckchair 'wallah' during summertime. As the weather darkened, I'd return home to my room, taking refuge in school days, followed by solitary evenings, pretending to do homework and sometimes actually doing some or postponing it until the morning bus. I had a sneaking suspicion that poverty would not become me later in life and some reluctant preparation had to be made for my future as a film director or pilot, or maybe doctor. After all, if my stupid but nice eldest sister, Sheila, had qualified as a doctor with plaudits then surely, I'd breeze it. Self-admiration was a necessary characteristic for a boy who had moved schools several times and had to establish himself anew amongst scrabbling strangers.

"Tinners Arms? When?"

"Next Tuesday, we're meeting Peter and some others. About noon? They close at three."

Ah good, Bungey will be less confrontational among friends; he'll tell his tales of seafaring years (all true, I reluctantly admit) and during a couple of pints, I can chat privately to Mother in the stone fireplace with room for only two. "Yes, I reckon so, see you there about one. Can you bring me a warm blanket? Don't tell Bungey; he'll accuse me of being queer if he hears I need a blanket in a climate as benign as Cornwall's. He'll tell me it's not Murmansk."

Mother laughed; she appreciated that I tolerated her man; he had some qualities but also some drawbacks, and I could hold my own while keeping my eye on distant ambitions outside of Cornwall. I replaced the phone. Cornwall was my love, but I knew it would become my cage if I became too old to escape. Moving school so much in Scotland, and then again in Cornwall, gave me a zest for life and its different peoples. So, pilot it is then, decision made!

The A30 road started in London and became less busy, narrower, foggier, wetter and more rural as it traversed Devon and Cornwall, reaching Sennen, finishing at Land's End as the fabled land of Lyonesse drops into the depths. My bike ride would take me two miles on the A30, then eleven miles on the B3306. How I loved the rises and corners of that agricultural road as I sped slightly unwisely from Sennen towards Zennor, a long and winding road complete with herds of cows and their smells, then becoming single track through working farms. Wet cow slurry would present a challenge to a speedy boy on a bike, with his tyre treads eternally awaiting replacement. By comparison, the view low down from a car between these granite hedges was like from a bobsleigh shuttling down the high-sided Cresta run, danger expected but unseen round every corner. However, atop a tractor, or astride a bike, gave an unsurpassed view of this ancient, quoit-bespeckled countryside, cairns of granite on sweeps of farmland and bracken. Small villages on the way gave a chance to buy a breakfast pasty, food of the gods, best held in one hand and a handlebar in the other. Pasties keep hot for hours. Declutching posed a problem, so then the pasty was kept close between the legs, but not too close! This part of West Penwith was home to the pasty, a rugged pastry that could be dropped down a mineshaft, from working wife to hungry hubby, without damage to the pasty but possibly some danger to the miners below. In mining areas, pasties were known as 'Cousin Jack's mouth organ'. The folk tales of pasty history were wry, funny, self-deprecatory and sometimes even true.

With 'Cousin Jack's mouth organ' now safely between my legs, these sharp corners, followed by sudden inclines, demanded the ideal gear when riding my underpowered bike. Keep up the speed and revs. Intimate knowledge of the turns and rises gave me pleasure in my self-adjudged mastery of the route. The joy of this subsided as I regretfully changed down, turning into the seven hundred-year-old Tinners Arms in the tiny hamlet of Zennor, alphabetically the last parish in Britain.

The local Wesleyan minister, Mr Wigley, was father to a boy in my class and, in a spirit of stupidity, we called him, asking in a deep voice, 'are you wiggly?" and upon his polite answer of, 'yes, I'm Wigley', we would howl and say, 'well, if you're wiggly, don't sleep on corrugated iron then'. It was only when older we realised that this, otherwise stern, gentleman was taking his kindly part in our happy humour. Good man. As I passed the chapel, I felt shamefaced at how often he must have had to endure this, but the Lord works in mysterious ways, he probably surmised as he despairingly shook his head.

Sure enough, there was Mother's Vauxhall Viva, parked in the road, her stated ambition always to be the car closest to the pub door. In West Penwith, strangely, parking alongside the road is almost encouraged as tractors cannot pass and have to ask in the pub for the offending owners of the higgledy-piggledy cars; this gives the tractor driver a chance to chat, explore the different ways everyone is related and grudgingly accept a drink. "Don't know if I should, but a pint'll do me," and generally distribute bonhomie, leaving with a laugh and a shout of, "You buggers'll be the end of me…" as everyone stomps out to rearrange their cars into a more pleasing pattern. The specific swear words used could neatly identify the farmers from the sailors, also the smell, 'parfum de Penwith' – I nicknamed it pointlessly as no one seemed to get the remark.

Tinners Arms, Zennor, credit Pauline Eccles

Into the Tinners Arms, ducking under the low, granite lintel built for Cornish piskies, I hear Mother and Bungey in the 'chair', with a well-honed tale of how Bungey accidentally sank a German ship in the foggy Channel two years after the war had finished. Much laughter, mainly from pals who had also been in the war and had swapped their well-worn tales before. All Bungey's stories were true and well-known, but the amusement was in the telling. "I tell ee, I got my own back on they buggers." His tales of adventure were backed up by old crewmen. During the North Atlantic convoys, his merchant ship had been sunk by a German pocket battleship, the *Von Scheer*, followed by another sinking a year later, torpedoed by a Japanese sub in the Pacific. Both sinkings resulted in three days and nights in open boats. Cornwall, with its history of fishing, smuggling and piracy, was a recruiting pool for these seamen: fishing, military and merchantmen.

Question: Why are all pirates from Cornwall?
Answer: Because they are-r-r-r-r.

A Cornishman's future was by accident of birth, mainly, and he became a miner, fisher or farmer, all hard work. Bungey had come from a landowning family but had run away, aged fifteen, to sea. "Books weren't for me." I'd once asked Bungey for the most horrible thing he'd seen in three sinkings and fifty years at sea. He answered, "Third mate died of syphilis comin' back from Murmansk," and said no more. Was this a salutary tale to warn me? He was ostentatiously outraged by my lifestyle but genuinely concerned about me too.

Now swaddled in our granite fireplace hidey-hole, whilst the others drank to excess, Mother waved her glass, trying to persuade me to pose as a model in her art classes. She had recently taken up portrait painting and seemed to have a previously undiscovered talent; her enthusiasm could conquer all challenges, with the notable exception of driving safely. Our drinks arrived via the neat waitress, whose complexion had clearly benefited from Zennor's milk farms. Mother took whisky, Glenfiddich as usual, and I took beer, good St Austell's ale, though I eyed her Glenfiddich for the next round.

Mother proposed the terms of my attendance. "So that's it, once a week, sail loft in Back Road West, St Ives, good view over Porthmeor Beach surf, just up your strand. We pay models £10 a session for two hours. Portrait painting."

I exhaled. "Portrait painting, that's a relief; I feared maybe 'Reclining Nudes', although the 'reclining' bit does have some attraction."

Her tolerant smile indicated she took my remark as a 'yes'. We were interrupted by Bungey, as usual 'three sheets to the wind', dropping his beer glass onto the granite flagstones; time stood still, the gang frozen in time and horror, as the dimpled beer tankard dropped to the flags, bouncing on its edge. Drunkenly, Bungey peered down to find it bouncing back upwards towards him, miraculously undamaged, beer still within. Instinctively, he caught it to rousing cheers.

"Six bells, time to go," announced Mother and rattled her car keys to the cheering drinkers. "See you all next Thursday."

After much backslapping and well-worn insults, this group of old pals spilled onto the road, slipping in cow pats and swearing above and beyond the necessity of the situation.

Art School modelling? I'd committed myself to every Wednesday morning for the next six weeks. I'll need my mate Alastair to fill some half-days for me – 'mair expense' gloomed my inner careful Scot.

Kissing Mother farewell and securing her thoughtful Dundee cake and slab of cheese on the fuel tank, I unsteadily bestrode my bike and wove its noisy exhaust off to the 'Land of the End'. Fittingly, Kernow is Cornish for Cornwall, coming from the Celtic word *kernou*, meaning 'horn' or 'headland'.

The weeks were already speeding by; there was surfing to be done, and I wished that every wave was never ending.

La pura vida.

4

Mid-summer 1969

Playing It Cool...

I strolled by the waters one evening so bright
And awaited the stars in the darkening night.

ME.

Halfway through the summer of '69 came my A-level results. I could barely remember doing my exams as six busy weeks at Sennen had since passed. I wasn't expecting to excel as I'd left my revising to the last fortnight, setting off to Mirren's house with a desperate plan of intense, last-minute revising over several days, a plan doomed to predictable failure. Guess what horror would sabotage my hopes? I'd loaded all my papers on my bike's pannier behind, 'secured' by an old bungee cord stretched to its limit of credibility. Riding in the evening gloom along Penzance's storm-damaged promenade – weaving round broken pieces of concrete, buffeted by wind and rain, sea spray ripping horizontally from the onshore wind and heavy surf – the bungee finally failed, and I lost all notebooks and notes off the bike pannier. I only noticed my papers after several hundred yards, as the streetlights caught the last sheets swirling mockingly in my wake. Screeching to a slithery halt, I looked back; cars were chewing up my scholastic salvation. Hope 'sinks' eternal in the human breast. I tried to salvage the remnants. Twisting and darting in the rain with all the ineptitude of an apprentice bullfighter, I avoided the oncoming cars and gathered the sodden remains. The ink of my fountain pen on the wet pages had blotted my future.

So, two months later, it was with hope and fear I ripped open my results letter, the envelope scrawled with two redirections. The Post Office had done well to find me on the beach; the letter had been posted to Mother, forwarded to Mirren, then forwarded – still unopened – to the café, where it sat propped against my pot of hot tea. Mrs Clifton had spotted me trudging across the beach, as I picked glass shards sparkling in the lower morning sun; better to pick up any glass than do a dozen first aid 'repairs' later in the day. She looked maternally at me as she busied herself setting the tables; she knew the other kids had received their letters last week and wondered at my silence. I wafted my envelope over my steaming tea and considered my scholastic desserts. What did I deserve after two years of frittering away my natural maths talents? I was seldom at school, generally away playing sport for the school, the town and the county. Our school greatly valued sport, so the headmaster, generally a disciplinarian, was extra lenient when a boy excelled at sport, and he delighted when we were county champions.

My form and maths teacher, Mr Mostyn, had laughed when looking over my shoulder during my S-level paper, but, but, but… against fear and dread, I had been awarded one A, two Ds and an extra S-level; that would be just enough for my uni offer. University of Southampton, here I come, armed with a generous council grant – thank you again, Cornwall, my lover, my dear, my flower!

Mrs Clifton dusted my table inquisitively. I smiled and said triumphantly, "Mrs Clifton, you are the first to know. Against all the odds and teacherly predictions, I've done it, just squeaked into my first choice: Southampton."

"Well done, boy, you'll go far, at least 110 miles if you don't get lost over Bodmin Moor," she laughed. "Your mother will be pleased."

"You know, Mrs Clifton, I don't really deserve this, but what a relief! My life of unmerited serendipity marches on."

"You're making me cry now." She smiled through affectionate tears. "Future beckons, I'd say."

Only slightly embarrassed at my good fortune, I exulted, "My ambition is to ultimately live a life of complete idleness and I'll stop at nothing to achieve it."

She laughed, flicking me affectionately with her handy tea towel. "Get back to your real work, now, my 'andsum."

"You call lifeguarding 'real work', boy? Har, har," shouted Mr Clifton, laughing through his pipe and coughing ash. Mrs Clifton smiled indulgently and wiped away the accumulating patina of pipe ash.

I loved Mrs Clifton's motherly ways, but I didn't deserve her generosity of spirit. I wafted a cheery wave behind me.

"Sandy is a great name for you. Always on the beach or in the surf. Hair and complexion colouring, too, what could be better?" I shouted to Sandy as she bounced along.

She came closer, releasing her dogs. "Well, it's really a nickname, cos of all that stuff. It started as a joke, then became natural, so I was 'appy an' I went along with it, see. Also, I like 'er, the singer like, Sandie Shaw, bare feet."

"Gosh, so what's your real name, then?"

"Gail."

"Gail? D'you mean G-a-i-l or G-a-l-e?"

She laughed. "Gail, but it sounds like a gale. Surname is Shaw."

"And so, your name is Sandy Shaw, sounds like Sandy Shore," I marvelled. Again, I wasn't sure whether I was being tricked again; everyone around here seemed to have names connected with the sea. Could it be coincidence? "Your dogs are Labradors; that's even a seaside name, Labrador," I ventured.

"Well, yes, but that's a happenstance; we was given one puppy so we bought another for company, similar breed like."

"So, do these beautiful dogs have names about the sea? Ruff and Smooth?" I suggested, stroking their healthy coats.

"Ha, ha. No, they're Don and Dee, like the rivers. Nice short, sharp names for dogs. Don's the boy an' 'e's black, colour of the peaty river in Aberdeen. Dee's the girl, means goddess in Roman, she's chalky an' a bit orangey. Colours like those rivers, my dad says, 'e was an angler, 'e was."

"Well, at least Derek's name is normal, but his surname is Clifton so that's just a bit 'river-ish', I suppose, Clifton Bridge in Bristol."

"Oh, 'im? Happens 'is real name is Eddie, like the singer Eddie Fisher. Mrs Clifton loved 'is singin', so she named 'im Eddie. Yes, it sounds like a river or beach eddy. Listen close, like, she calls 'im Eddie at times, affectionate, she's the only one oo can do that."

"Fantastic, I'll rib him endlessly about Eddie, eddy."

"I wouldn't, the last joker at school got a broke nose. Ee gets teasy as an adder if you calls 'im Eddie," she advised.

"So, how come he's called Derek?" I pried.

Sandy relaxing with her beautiful dogs and a pal, 1969

"Cos ee always says 'dreckly', real Cornish like for 'directly', when he means now or sometimes never. So, they nicknamed 'im Derek, like 'Dreckly.'"

I stood, wondering if I was in a comedy play with made-up names. What about John in the car park? Was it short for Jonah? Sandy whistled her dogs and was gone.

Working on a beach changes perspective. Naturally, weather is important, individual days not so much, and 'next Wednesday' crept up behind my alarm clock to surprise me. A sleepy stagger across the beach to the public toilets, a quick wash and an affectionate check of my bike led me to an early morning zoom along the winding A30 bends, the sun rising over my right shoulder and cows trudging back from their milking, leaving their wet slurry to catch the unwary motorcyclist. Most places in Cornwall have two names: the original name from the Cornish Brythonic language, and its anglicised name. Thus, St Ives, as you will know it in English, is made up from the Cornish *Porth-ia* of porth, meaning 'harbour, cove' and Ia, an Irish saint. Who is Saint Ia, then, I know you'll ask. Well, she floated over from Ireland to Cornwall (Kernow) on a millstone or a cabbage leaf (it may have been a coracle; I hear you floating this shape-associating idea).

My bike knew well its route, so I tried to remember the little poem of St Ives, overpopulated with fish-guzzling cats.

As I was going to St. Ives,
I met a man with seven wives,
Each wife had seven sacks,
Each sack had seven cats,
Each cat had seven kits,
Kits, cats, sacks, and wives,
How many were going to St. Ives?

And the answer is 'one'.

I arrived early in Porthia (St Ives) and had already introduced myself to the small group of elderly, expiring and aspiring artists, before Mother arrived in a swirl of chiffon scarf and a wave of cigarette holder. I coughed politely and pointedly. "We only smoke at the break and windows shall be opened," Mother reassured me.

The 'small group' welcomed me, and I turned my chair, ensuring it faced the surf beach of Porthmeor, a surfing alma mater for me. "The light will fall better from that direction," I assured them. The studio was previously a fisherman's gloomy sail loft – part of several terraced lofts – most now converted, with broad windows replacing the wooden shutters, giving an elevated light-flooded prospect onto Porthmeor's beach. The 'small group' fussed, discussed my beard and army surplus jacket, again checked the light was falling correctly and finally agreed that everyone in their semicircle had an interesting view of my cheery face, temporarily set sphinx-like. They examined me closely, prodded my hair, discussed my eye colour, measured my ears with palette brushes and crept silently up to assess my 'very Scottish' skin tones, which Mother assured them was due to a healthy, Ayrshire diet and fresh, gale-force air. They would later discover my skin would tan as the season progressed until I took on a 'pleasing honey colour', Mother again. Everyone was eventually satisfied, and their earnest hobby progressed with occasional whispers, interrupted by nesting herring gulls on the slate roof, occasionally dislodging the residue of two hundred years, dispensing a shimmer of dust and droppings. Don't breathe in; only breathe out, I silently advised myself.

An elderly gentleman, ignoring the no-smoking rule, leant over, peered over his greasy specs, breathed an aura of sunlit pipe smoke in my face and complained about my pose.

"Don't move," shrieked the others. "We've already sketched in his 'essentials.'"

"I thought this was portraiture!" I blurted, worrying that 'essentials' might be an artistic euphemism, determining to check their easels as soon as the tea break.

After one hour, a break was announced, and I was allowed a toilet stop and coffee 'n' bickies. Having a few minutes to observe their efforts, I now circled the easels; don't trip now, face expressionless. Summoning my so-far-unused great tact and diplomacy, "I see you've caught my regal expression," a touch of humour suppressed my urge to cackle helplessly. Perhaps some are unintentional devotees of Salvador Dali, I feared. Or was I really as unattractive as that? It's unusual to have a cheekbone in profile. With huge relief, I found that most were truly terrible; some were passable; and Mother's was best, thankfully. I still have hers, hidden in my attic, Dorian Gray-like. Despite these cack-handed strivings, nonetheless the teacher persevered with supportive comments. I continued stalking, my harsh assessments hidden behind cheery remarks of encouragement about fine hair texture or the difficulty of painting curls. I realised after the second hour ended that I was becoming tired by sitting; I'd never really been absolutely still in my life, finding it exhausting, especially today when yet another 'artist' measured my nose. "Aquiline or Roman?" came the aired queries, followed by companionable guffaws. After the two hours, my ennui and knee twitching, caused by immobility, was swiftly dispelled by the proffered £10 which came in coins various. Art clearly didn't pay, for these elderly students at least. Mother hovered to ensure that I accepted their saucer of coins and graciously, too. Pouring it all into the oil-stained pockets of my army surplus jacket, I decided to save carefully for uni, just in case the scurrilous rumours of Olympian beer-drinking were true.

After handshaking and backslapping and reassuring all of my willingness to return next week, I fled into the fresh air. Thanking Mother; she thanking me; me warning her about smoking; she promising unconvincingly to give up, we parted and I sped up Porthmeor Hill – casting a backwards glance at the beach – and out of St Ives before the morning grockle crush clogged its narrow cobblestone arteries. I reflected on one of my Porthmeor Beach surfing wipeouts, hitting the hard-packed, sandy bottom, unconscious and coming to being mulled gently in a froth of sandy water, waves cuddling me. Later, I had decided that dying semi-conscious in the shoreline surf was not frightening but calming: mother's womb, warm baths, floating in a continuum of flow. Some philosophies see death as a passage to a better life.

Though the waves leap, soft shall ye sleep, Ocean's a royal bed.
TRADITIONAL NONSENSE POEM,
AUTHOR UNKNOWN, 18TH CENTURY.

Putting the sun over my left shoulder, the bike returned me to the windswept, most westerly parish in Britain.

The artistic 'small group' had asked that I keep my hair the same length, a tricky task as hair grows rapidly in summer's warm embrace. Visiting a barber was out of the question, too expensive, and I had no chance of leaving work during a barbershop's opening times. The solution came: put on your crash helmet and then scissor the extruding, offending hair; think Garfunkel, and gravity can take care of the top as the hair just becomes denser.

My sister Fiona had started visiting Sennen, as her latest boyfriend, Tom, and his two brothers, were surfers. I knew them well from before, good guys all. Their family were prosperous builders so all three had vans and petrol. Instantly popular with we surfers who had neither; everyone would pile boards into their vans and hurtle to wherever was deemed the best surf conditions that day, propelled by the radio blasting the Beach Boys or Jan and Dean.

The warmth of our sun,
Caresses these western shores.

ME.

Sister Fiona, glamourous and adventurous, 1969.

Fiona had called, asking me to meet her at the Old Success; Tom was getting the beers, we two awaiting him in the car park's late-afternoon sun. Fiona was in challenging mood. "You can't keep every secret from me, ha, you must be sleeping with Mirren; I know cos you stay at her house and you were bringing her to school on your motorbike."

"Does Mother know?"

"Well, yes, she heard it from Mirren's mother."

"Mirren's mum is an alcoholic, charming nonetheless, but not the most reliable source of information."

41

"You were banned from bringing Mirren on your smelly motorbike into the Girls School, and it dripped oil."

"Yes, true, but then I started dropping her outside and dripping in the street."

"You'd have been banned from that too, as the Head Girl was complaining to the Head Mistress." Fiona knew this as she was a prefect.

"Then I would have dropped her further away, but now it's the end of term and *summertime and the living is easy...*" I crooned mockingly.

"Well, everyone knows, anyway."

"Has Mirren said anything?"

"No."

"Then no one really knows for sure."

"They can draw their own conclusions."

"Then they're drawing exactly that, their *own* conclusions."

"Anyway, I hate you cos you sleep with all my friends, say nothing, they say nothing cos you asked them to say nothing, then you take the moral high ground when I need to know what's going on."

"You're using a callous tone in your search for secrets, dear sister, so you'll be unsuccessful. Anyway, it's impossible to sleep with all your friends because you have too many friends and only some are sufficiently attractive."

"Well, it's true – you are sleeping with her."

"You didn't hear it from me."

"Ha, you slept with Jane at the County Doubles at Perranporth."

"Well, I suppose it's all in the name: Doubles, but I also was in the Singles and you don't accuse me of masturbation."

"You could at least tell me if you slept with Jane; she's one of my best friends."

"Did Jane tell you we were together?"

"Not as such, but she's been asking after you. I heard you and Bonzo shared a tent, and Jane and her friend had a tent next to yours in the same campsite, so it's clear to me. She said you all got drunk."

"Hmmm, not definitive proof."

"Well, if you didn't, then just deny it and it's settled."

"I can't do that cos then you'll start to try by elimination to divide your friends into 'those denied' and 'those not denied', then you'll draw your own conclusions and present your gossip as truth."

"Tom and I are going to the US in summer."

"Wow, that's a real non sequitur! Does Mother know?"

"No, it's a secret; only Sandy and you know."

"Ahaa, so you've told me and Sandy. Sandy hasn't mentioned it; I'll say nothing, so effectively the only person who can't keep your secret is you."

"You're soooo sarcastic."

"I think you'll find that was irony. Anyway, does Tom know he's going to the US this summer?"

"Not yet, I'll tell him later that we're going, ha, ha."

"Here he comes now with the drinks. You'd better tell him soon as I'd heard that all three brothers, Tom, Mark, and Al, are going surfing in Biarritz this summer."

"God! Why didn't he tell me? The secretive bastard."

"I'm not sure Tom knows yet as his brothers just decide for him and they do all the planning. Eventually, he'll need to decide between Biarritz, that he doesn't yet know about, and America, that he also doesn't yet know about. What a choice: a holiday with you versus a summer's surfing in Biarritz." Fiona gave me a venomous glare. Beer now in hand, "Cheers, Tom, your good health, wealth and mysterious future."

Tom looked puzzled but guzzled his beer, drowning the stresses of being Fiona's boyfriend. The sun was setting over Cape Cornwall, crepuscular sunbeams radiating a spectacular sunset as we contemplated our respective secrets, little knowing the three very separate life tracks we would actually take. I was reminded of a poem I tried to write at school:

The tide full in, the sun setting over glittering water,
and rays sparkling off Neptune's peeling wave crests.
NOT DEATHLESS POETRY.

"Anyway, how's Bruce these days? I used to fancy him." Another non sequitur from Fiona, oblivious to Tom's ignominy. I knew my sister would then start to loudly list her previous boyfriends in order of quality. These previous boyfriends could, unbeknown to them, score points according to wealth, sexual ability, charm, sense of humour and desirability.

To save Tom's embarrassment, I cut her short. "Bruce is fine, I've heard. Surf is forecast big tomorrow morning. I'm going out early; Tom, are you brothers-three coming over?" I said, quickly closing down Fiona's conversation to save Tom's further discomfort. It was getting late; we all gazed at the building surf, the sun dozing towards Cape Cornwall.

The Sun's rim dips; the stars rush out;
At one stride comes the dark...
SAMUEL TAYLOR COLERIDGE,
THE RIME OF THE ANCIENT MARINER.

Ah, yes, Bruce, fondly remembered by Fiona. At age sixteen and seventeen, I was working the summertimes during my school holidays at St Ives's Porthgwidden Beach as loyal assistant to Bruce in my role as assistant deckchair 'wallah'. Bruce was a drug partaker, still relaxed mornings but alert by lunchtime. Fortunately for him, I used to sleep at the beach in our deckchair shed, washing in the public toilets too, all good practice for Sennen. I'd open our shed after 9am and by 11am I'd already have rented out all the deckchairs and windbreaks and trousered my tips, depositing some for Bruce as a 'tithe' to my overlord. He would grunt his acceptance through his foggy hangover and show his graciousness by buying the first round later that evening. He set a useful example of how to charm girls and I paid close attention to his pointers over a few pints of black and tan.

Bruce was well-read, a fan of Jack Kerouac and other drug-addled Beat writers. Kerouac was still alive then but died, predictably young, in 1969, aged forty-seven. He died from an abdominal haemorrhage caused by a lifetime of heavy drinking, not, amazingly, drug-taking, though that probably didn't help. On briefly meeting Bruce six years later, we discussed Kerouac again. "Not so much 'On the Road' as 'On the Slab', I suppose," I joked unsympathetically. Bruce told me he himself was in the process of changing his ways. I had confidence Bruce would manage that, his real first loves were several beers followed by free love; he was remarkably successful in this, being tall, good-looking and a girl magnet. Despite me being only sixteen, as Bruce's close pal, I benefited from the serendipitous 'fallout' of superfluous girlfriends. Bruce's preferred beer was a black and tan: a half-pint of bitter topped up with a bottle of Guinness. As you're part way down the glass, you can order another bottle of Guinness which changes the composition. I asked the endlessly knowledgeable Bruce why it was called a black and tan. Was it just the colours of beer and stout? He explained it was the nickname given to the British paramilitaries, made up of English and Irish WWI veterans, formed to suppress the Irish Independence movement in the early 1920s. These 'Black and Tans' employed brutal actions in an attempt to suppress the IRA's guerrilla war, massacring Irish civilians and burning towns. They were called the 'Black and Tans', having khaki military trousers and darker police uniform shirts.

Thus, Black and Tan is a pejorative term in Ireland and calling someone a Black and Tan is a deep insult at worst and, at best, is considered culturally ignorant. In Ireland, one should consider ordering a half-and-half instead: half Guinness and half Harp Lager, making it all Irish. So, we had several long arguments about this; I insisted on drinking it only if ordered as a half-and-half. Bruce secretly agreed, but I suspected he'd only introduced the term to show an educational advance on me.

In St Ives in the '60s, I was known as the 'normal guy', which in itself was an ironic comment on my abnormality in a town of artists, folksingers, potters, poets and dropouts. For me, life was lots of sport, no smoking (several relatives had died of cancer, and I hated the idea of paying to speed my future demise) and no drugs (I saw too many pals lose their personality to the subsequent sloth). When asked about this, 'you want to live forever?', I used to reply with the old joke, 'I want to live until 120 and then be shot by a jealous lover'. Druggies often laugh for no reason but don't get jokes, even though jokes generally illustrate an underlying truth.

In some other ways, I was also regarded as abnormal. Sartorially, I sported ripped, bleached Levis and an orange leather waistcoat. How many times did passers-by offer to buy that waistcoat off my back? I always refused but did eventually sell it in 1973 in Barbados to an American for a large sum. A good profit considering my sister had chucked it out years ago; I'd snaffled it and cut off the 'cowboy' fringes, wearing it bare-chested!

Sporting my orange waistcoat and torn Levis, one morning I was wandering to work, walking past the Sloop Inn on St Ives's waterfront at 9.30am, when I was accosted by the Sloop Inn's landlord, new and fiercely determined to set standards.

"You're not coming in here," he shouted at me.

"Correct, you're not open till half past ten," I smugly responded.

"Your types are unwelcome!" he raged as he intercepted me outside on the cobbled street. "You're just a beatnik, a weirdo. Everything's changed here now; this is a proper pub." Is this a record, to be chucked out of a pub whilst not being in it? I continued strolling past, heading for Porthgwidden Beach. "So, tell your pals," starting to foam, he shouted at my back.

"I'm more likely to tell the brewery, Mr Landlord."

I didn't tell the brewery, but after two weeks of low takings during peak summer, he was out. The Sloop resumed its mix of pipe-sucking fishermen, superannuated beatniks, lost hippies and wide-eyed tourists; the till was ringing again! Normality had been restored and peace confidently bestrode the land.

I saw Bruce again, only once after my two years of being attentive to his kindly instruction in the importance of hedonism, but I had learned his lessons well.

Play in the ocean of awareness.
BRUCE.

5

Autumn 1969

Our Sunshine Is Slipping Away...

O the opal and the sapphire of that wandering western sea.
THOMAS HARDY, A LOVER OF CORNWALL. *BEENY CLIFF.*

As the summer wore nicely on, I'd begun to know the locals, some lifeboatmen in the pub, some who also did occasional work for Derek. The weeks were speeding by and uni at Southampton loomed in my nervous dreams. Living in a city? Not my style really, but 'here goes nothing'. I needed to say goodbye to Mirren; our closeness was intermittent and we were starting to drift apart. She'd changed her name to Morven at her friend's suggestion. Morven was said to mean mermaid in Cornish from *mor* 'sea' and *voren* 'maiden' – it was associated with the Mermaid of Zennor. Her mother was predictably angered as she had chosen Mirren, Gaelic for 'drop of the sea', almost the same name, but now Morven it is.

What would happen? I didn't know, but we both knew we had different experiences with drugs and vastly different friends.

There was always a gaggle of girls and a plethora of pals around my hut if the weather was good. Naturally, in those dope fiend days, I had to discourage smoking near my hut without losing friends so I'd shoo them away to distant dunes. Did I smoke? No. Did I want a conviction for drugs before becoming a pilot? Also, no.

My lifeguarding was now over until summer 1970, but I could still use my hut until I handed in the key, keeping two copies 'just in case'. I needed to visit Morven as she had a day off from her waitressing, but my bike's clutch was awaiting spare parts; a dodgy clutch has never reached the top of Sennen Hill. So, I hitch-hiked to the small village of Paul, knowing Morven's mother would be collapsing into her van at exactly 2.30pm, after drinking-up time. There was no direct road from Sennen to Paul village and, hitching by two cars and the 'running board' of a tractor, I reached the King's Arms pub in Paul with twenty minutes to spare. Best to stay sober as Morven's mum would not be. I wandered through the graveyard, killing time. Graveyards in Cornwall are interesting places. I spotted the grave of Dolly Pentreath (*pentreath*: head of the beach), famed for being the last person to speak and scold in the Cornish language, her native tongue. Dolly died in 1777, after uttering her last words, '*My ny vynnav kewsel Sowsnek!*' ('I will not speak English!'). By reputation, Dolly was an indomitable woman and so was Morven's mum, whom I could now hear being hustled out towards her van. Everyone knew she had suffered great tragedy years ago when her son had died in a collision with a car and 'allowances were made'. She had taken to the 'gargle' as the Irish say, but she showed great courage in bringing up two fostered Nigerian boys, little Bayo and Fola. Luckily, the pub closing time allowed her time to sober up before the boys returned from primary school. This timing meant I knew exactly when to cadge a lift.

"Hello, Mrs Shires, how are you this beautiful afternoon?" I greeted her.

She shook the rain drops from her headscarf, an unsteady smile wreathing her face. "Kenneth, I'm delighted to see you, beautiful afternoon or not."

I hugged her warmly, a wonderful lady. "I'm on the scrounge for a lift to see Morven."

"Certainly. Drive me home, young man, and be quick about it." She laughed, handing me the keys.

"Sorry, cannot, still only got a bike license, so far."

"Pedantic youth," she said, indicating the passenger seat. "Well, strap yourself in!" she ordered, despite her antiquated estate car not having seat belts fitted. Morven's mum, weaving drunkenly in the old Hillman van, lurched onto the road. I braced myself; only ten minutes of terror awaited.

She appeared to be trying single-handedly to persuade the rest of the country to drive on the opposite side of the road. Sweden had managed this switch five years previously but only after a herculean effort of planning and education to prepare their population. Everyone knew our tiny band of local police turned a blind eye provided she kept out of Penzance but eventually, after a crash which blocked the road, she was banned. Everyone breathed a sigh of relief but, nothing daunted, she took to a horse-and-buggy. This was an inadvertent advantage as all her trips were less than five miles and she could tether it to the newly installed parking meters in Penzance, paying nothing, money saved. Threats from thwarted traffic wardens would follow but eccentrics are humoured, yay even admired, in West Penwith, especially when frustrating officialdom. "Well, the sign doesn't mention buggies, my good man." Morven's mum would opine happily and the traffic warden would feign false rage and shake a friendly fist. Visitors were enchanted by characterful Cornwall and thrilled that an elderly woman could still 'cock a snook' at authority. The only participant upset was Morven's riding horse, strapped-up, unsuited to buggies and facing the struggle up Paul Hill with shopping and some essential 'gargle' aboard.

I said goodbye to Morven during that slightly distant weekend and returned to Sennen to pack. With my sparse, worldly possessions aboard, minus my surfboard, I dropped by at Mother's house. Before this first trip to uni, Bungey felt the need to celebrate my departure from Cornwall by pouring monster whiskies for the three of us and retelling sea stories. Time passed and darkness had fallen as I left Mother's house, in a shower of rain and cascading autumn leaves. By now, Bungey had consumed the required amount to become aggressive. "You're worse than your bloody brother," he bellowed, badgering me onto the driveway.

As I left with a disrespectful laugh, I shouted my most used, sarcastic insult over my shoulder: "I'll take that as a compliment, sailor." Now, this is known in French as *l'esprit de l'escalier* (or the spirit of the stairway, as you deliver your crushing insult whilst leaving, thus allowing no time for your opponent to reply). Of course, this only works if you actually leave. In this case, I mounted my bike, casually booting the kick-starter but with no result. He was following me, delivering additional insults with a salty flavour, working himself into further paroxysms of threats. I resorted to pushing my bike along the drive in the dark, leaping on as it rolled down the gentle slope. We continued in a comedy of stupidity: he was bellowing colourful insults in my right ear; I was trying to ignore him and diagnose the problem – *yes*, I had it; the fuel was turned off (a common error). A quick kick again and "Brrrooooommmmm." Away I sped, shouting my own inferior and pointless insults to the four winds.

During my journeys on the A30, Bodmin Moor featured as an obstacle of mythical might. Rain, high winds, slippery surface, leaves and mud, all to be battled in the dark with my vibrating six-volt headlight flickering. Stunted hawthorn waved into the road and pecked at my helmet as my underpowered bike struggled on the inclines. Forgotten poems would invade my befuddled mind:

> *The wind was a torrent of darkness among the gusty trees.*
> *The moon was a ghostly galleon tossed upon cloudy seas.*
> *The road was a ribbon of moonlight over the purple moor,*
> *And the highwayman came riding—*
> *Riding—riding—*
> *The highwayman came riding, up to the old inn-door.*
> ALFRED NOYES, *THE HIGHWAYMAN*, 1906.

Passing the night light outside Daphne du Maurier's Jamaica Inn, I celebrated that I'd reached halfway and dreaded the remaining ten moorland miles with the dark night drizzling in the headlight's cyclops gaze. A BSA C15 motorbike is designed to teach you many things: humility (the ability to withstand friends' cackling insults); resilience (pushing it uphill in Cornish horizontal rain); mechanical learning (lots of practice); parsimony (no need to spend on a worthless bike); optimism (one day I'll buy a better bike); and stoicism (for the moment I couldn't afford anything better). A C15 has only one noticeable advantage: there is no need to lock it as no one would wish to steal it, and anyway, it was not fitted with a lock, cos if it had been, then it wouldn't have worked for sure.

First day at uni, as I coasted past the square block of Montefiore Hall of Residence, there was a huddle of students and police cars, everyone alternately casting their heads downwards and then upwards. What had happened? An ambulance screeched to a halt, doors opening and paramedics bursting forth, an inauspicious start of term. A second-year had committed suicide from the high-rise building; he couldn't face the new term and tragically threw himself out of his window. Suicides on day one? Not an encouraging start for me, a new student.

I stupidly approached uni like I'd approached school, lots of sport and almost no studying. I played footie for the second XI, hung out at the bar, became table football champion (and again for the subsequent three years,

Wintry Southampton University in the snow, from top of the Maths Building

oh glory me, damning my inadequate CV). Strangely, my main friends had both failed a year, dropped out and then dropped in again this year. I met Dave Tanswell (a Jesus Christ lookalike), who busied himself with cars and civil engineering and Steve, who had spent last summer in Atlantic City gambling dens and had become a card sharp. He now saw the point of maths and financed his life by playing poker in the Students Union bar. Dave and Steve were not a pair of the highest achievers but were much better than me and they were focused if belatedly. I was most definitely not.

I made a weekend trip just before Christmas, over Bodmin Moor, down to see Morven in Newlyn. It was colder than normal with little to do. Morven was still at school, and I stayed at her mother's house with her mother's two delightful little fostered Nigerian boys, Bayo and Fola. Morven's mother received their fostering payments as a modest income. During the day, I would take Bayo, and alternately Fola, for rides on my bike along the local lanes. They loved this, Bayo's little face radiating both fear and anticipation if his turn was next. He would drag his brother Fola off the bike and leap on, ill-fitting helmet slanting on his dense curls, bright eyes peering out, reminding me of Burns's phrase: 'An' forward, tho' I canna see, I guess an' fear!'.

Then, with these few days over, back to uni. I saw the forecasts of a rare, advancing snow front that would cover Devon and parts of Cornwall, so I booked a train ticket – Penzance, Exeter, Southampton – and loaded my bike into the guard's van. I couldn't know that at Launceston, before Exeter, the train would load enough Christmas trees to bury my bike. Readying to get off at Exeter, I entered the guard's van and saw only trees. Asking the guard to hold the train, he helpfully replied, "We've got a schedule; you'll 'ave to clear the wagon en route and get off at Salisbury." As he prepared to blow his whistle, I took my chance and commenced hurling small trees onto the platform; he chucked them back on, but this is where fitness helps: I could throw out faster than he could throw in. I'd cleared a space, found my bike and, with a warning roar, jumped the gap onto the platform, scattering the guard sideways. I slithered on the blown snow and sped off. Good fun if you don't get caught, but I still had to sneak onto the next Southampton train later, hopefully from a different platform. My mood deepened approaching Southampton; uni did not become me and I faced two and a half years to go. Still, the Christmas break was approaching and perhaps a better opportunity with Morven.

At Christmas, Morven and I unwisely became engaged, after leaving the Union pub, and we visited the local jewellers for a beautiful ring, the fruits of my summer's pleasant labour.

So bonnie lassie bright and fair
Will ye be mine for ever mair.
'DUMBARTON'S DRUMS' (TRAD. FOLK SONG).

Aha, the joys of love with no eye to the future! Later, with Morven on the pillion, riding my bike up the steep Paul Hill in this winter's rare Cornish snow, we met a Land Rover coming down sideways and thus blocking the road as it descended. I couldn't stop as we would lose momentum, be hit by the Land Rover and never reach Morven's house at the top, so I weaved onto the gritted pavement. We passed round the descending Land Rover, laughing into the night. I was eighteen; Morven was sixteen; we were in temporary love and everything was possible.

When I told Mother about our engagement, she just burst out in uncontrollable laughter. I complained, "Most parents would say, 'Congratulations, dear.'" Mother laughed again. She was right; Morven and I were opposites but weirdly with a magnetic attraction. Her interests were music, art and the crowd who smoked dope. I was into sport, surfing and open air. This would never work. I was ridiculous; however, that was an especially romantic Christmas, not to be missed or forgotten in the clutter of later life. A month afterwards, we were unengaged, vacant almost.

Morven was still in school, working part-time in a Mousehole restaurant. She'd started smoking dope and her new friends had developed the laid-back attitude of 'I'm going to do something really interesting far away but not just yet'. The 'not just yet' lasts their whole lifetime. I never flagged my intended future; I just did it and seized opportunities. So, Morven and I grew apart; she even asked her cute friend to 'take Kenny over'. Said friend tried in very seductive ways, but I was only interested in Morven; maybe I found her remote attitude a challenge, but she was slipping away and we both knew it.

In February 1970 when I called her from Southampton, having queued for the only payphone in Hall, she finally made it too clear to avoid. "It's the end." In time-honoured fashion, in great distress, I mounted my bike in the rain and drove with tears in my eyes, singing, "Terry, Terrereee," the biker who drove to his death. Suicide is highly recommended in these situations, the only solution.

And I think on two bright eyes, and the melting mouth below
She's my beauteous nighean ruadh, She's my joy and sorrow too
And although she is untrue, well I cannot live without her
For my heart's a boat in tow, and I'd give the world to know
Why she means to let me go, as I sing horee, horo.
'THE LOCH TAY BOAT SONG' (TRAD. FOLK SONG).

As I sped, with a broken heart, through empty streets, I realised that driving at midnight in the rain through well-lit city streets is actually good fun. Maybe I should take up her friend's generous offer? The slim, cute, wriggly friend who loved to wrestle on the bed when Morven was out – yes, there's plenty more fish in the sea and summer's coming; when better to land a few fish? Holding a live mackerel in your wet hand is, after all, a very sensuous feeling of muscle and texture. Tears dried, I assessed that Morven liked to act cool and pursue a life of doing not very much. My way was action. The solution: a bit of work, pass exams, retain my council grant and 'the world is my lobster'. Most would say 'oyster', but lobsters are bigger and better and tastier, too, especially with a Rose Marie sauce, and where better to find a Rose Marie than on a summer beach? And summer approacheth; it's only February, but I could already feel the swells of June.

6

Early Summer 1970

And the Girls Are All So Tanned...

She appeared like an angel in feature and form.
'ROAD TO DUNDEE' (TRAD. FOLK SONG).

Well, the winter was history and summer cometh, optimism filling the landscape. Our group of pals at uni often went to jazz or folk evenings, but definitely no morris dancing. Hazel was at teacher training in Southampton and played the guitar. She arranged that I meet her friend Helen from St Buryan, near Sennen, during Easter break. My general problem was that I was open and friendly to girls, and they were often puzzled why I didn't ask them out. It never occurred to me to ask a girl out, which would weirdly pique her interest, until I was manoeuvred into an inescapably romantic situation and then I was cornered. The phrase, 'oh, I didn't realise you were interested' must have passed my dozy lips many times. Hazel arranged that I should meet this stranger, Helen, dancing at a party, and when I saw her across the room, instant attraction, a wonderful girl.

So now I'll sing to you, about a maiden fair,
I met the other evening in the corner of the square.
She had a dark and a roving eye, she was a charming rover,
And we rode all night, through the pale moonlight
Away down to Lamorna.
'LAMORNA' (TRAD.)

54

One Beauty and two Beasts

"Hello, I'm Kenny, a uni friend of Hazel's – maybe she mentioned me?"

"Awright then, yes, that's me, 'elen."

"Oh, Ellen?"

"No, H-Helen, with an aitch: Helen."

"OK, got it, like Helen of Troy, 'the face that launched a thousand ships.'"

"Yes, somethin' like that." She smiled and looked down.

She was hypnotically beautiful, the daughter of a local farmer. Silky hair, clear eyes, perfect skin, an ideal mix of ancient Celts and passing Spanish buccaneers. Milk and the farm life gave her a peaches-and-cream complexion, which contrasted with her glossy, jet-black hair. She had the glow of a government health advert in 'glorious technicolour', bizarrely often carrying a milking stool, her badge of a farmer's girl. She once encouraged me to try milking. The cows were not impressed and dried up at my cack-handed touch; however, Helen calmed them and could achieve maximum yield.

> *Her eyes are like the gleam,*
> *o' the sunlight on the stream*
> *And the song the fairies sing,*
> *seems like songs she sings at milking*
> 'THE LOCH TAY BOAT SONG'.

Everywhere we travelled together she would take her three-legged milking stool, a much-used symbol of her family of dairy farmers, who were all wonderful people, but they disapproved of me, and their judgement would be later proved correct, to my remorse.

End of spring term, I rocketed my recent purchase, a Triumph Tiger T350, down the A30, through the descending darkness, post-exam tiredness encroaching. I spotted the Jamaica Inn was open; here I could eat, down a swift pint at the Inn and sleep on my motorbike in the car park. The rain was stotting off the cobbles as I approached, and *The Highwayman* verses assailed me:

> *Over the cobbles he clattered and clashed in the dark inn-yard.*
> *He tapped with his whip on the shutters, but all was locked and barred.*
> *He whistled a tune to the window, and who should be waiting there*
> *But the landlord's black-eyed daughter,*
> *Bess, the landlord's daughter,*
> *Plaiting a dark-red love-knot in her long, black hair.*
> ALFRED NOYES, *THE HIGHWAYMAN.*

A hot pasty and two pints of St Austell ale later, I moved my bike to the darkest corner of the cobbles and 'so to bed'. My favoured sleeping method was propping it on its stand, sliding under its big, plastic cover and sleeping whilst sitting astride the bike, with my head and chest lying on the fuel tank. Can I hear a nightingale? According to my stepfather, Bungey, there's a Cornish miners' song, 'Sweet Nightingale':

> *You shall hear the fond tale,*
> *Of the sweet nightingale,*
> *As he sings in those valleys below.*

Bungey said only lovelorn nightingale males sing at night, to those females who are flying overhead while on migration. So, was this apt for me?
Awakening cold and damp on this June morning, no nightingales, only crows cawing as they flurried from the trees. Even in the shelter of this drystane dyke, I could feel the south-west wind gusting at forty knots. This is bound to be a buffeting ride to St Ives and then on to Sennen with my surfboard newly strapped on. The wind had dropped and visibility cleared as I approached

Sennen Village and prepared to descend into the cove. Stopping to look towards Scilly, I could see the islands standing tall, even the islands normally beyond the horizon were clearly visible with their images 'floating' above them. Bishop Rock lighthouse stood twice as high as normal. How could this be? Even a tanker passing off Land's End was stretched upwards, twice as tall. I figured it would be an optical illusion, but what? Descending the hill, I spotted Derek; as a fisherman, he must know; it wouldn't be the first illusion seen here.

"Soo-oo-ooh," sucked Derek with a rising tone. "Folks do say you can see St Agnes Island on Scilly sometimes; I've seen it myself, but I dunno!" he said, and thoughts of money to the fore, he asked, "Give me an 'and tomorrow morning, mackerel are running. There'll be a bit for you. Leavin' at six sharp with the tide, bad weather coming 'bout nine."

"Hey Derek, another question, bit topical, are you interested in this Cornish Independence movement?"

"Dunno, do they reckon it'll turn a profit?"

"They're thinking more of Cornish sovereignty, like when Cornwall had its own language and its own parliament, the Stannary."

"If they don't know 'bout its profits then tidn't much cop." He turned back to prepare his lines and hooks, beckoned by the season.

I busied myself settling back in my hut. During the past seven months, sand had deposited itself in small, well-defined hillocks and sand dust layered my stretcher bed. Much sweeping and dusting to be done but first a celebratory cup of tea in the sunshine of early morn, with a few minutes glorying in the joy of my splendid good fortune to be hired again for summer 1970.

I checked the red lifeline phone (not yet reconnected by the council), stowed my gear and wandered off to pick up my new beach logbook, sent by the council to Mrs Clifton in the café. The early season was cooler but clearer than usual, lots of dog walkers and strollers, but the high-pressure area meant little surf, so the beach was clear of surfers. Most swimmers judged the sea too cold this early in the season. I occasionally puzzled over my new optical illusion, but it would have to wait until I could reach Penzance library. No one local could shed any light, even with an encyclopaedia. I would sit at the café and chat to the Clifton family during their breaks; Mr Clifton was an avid weather-watcher and he forecast a storm coming overnight, into tomorrow and the following day. The newspaper's pressure chart confirmed his fears and Derek worried about ice-cream sales. "Bad weather, bad sales," he moaned.

Mr Clifton, Derek's father, was a man of gentle, warm humour, disciplined by a lifetime of army, work and duty; he swore only once in the four years I knew him – that occasion would be tomorrow and leave Mr Clifton shaking with a boiling fury at the narrowly avoided loss of an innocent child.

Who walkedst on the foamy deep,
And calm amidst its rage didst sleep;
O hear us when we cry to Thee,
For those in Peril on the sea.
HYMN: 'ETERNAL FATHER, STRONG TO SAVE'.

Tomorrow's weather came earlier than forecast, so no fishing. I'd heard the wind howling during the night and I woke up to thundering waves and storm-tossed foam blowing past my hut. It was both terrible and beautiful to behold, a heavy swell thundering in, wind strong onshore, powerful rip currents draining the spent surf and sand off the beach in rivers of our white sand heading seawards. I had closed the beach immediately when the conditions had awoken me. Red crossed flags forbid the unwary to enter the water, and now I was happily doing a crossword, surveying an empty beach and exchanging a few light-hearted words with Mr and Mrs Clifton, sitting at their café's balcony. Even Derek was away doing something clever with creels in his shed and improving his small, long-lining, mackerel boat. I was the only customer today and a pretty feeble customer, too. Mrs Clifton brought a large pot of tea and yesterday's cakes. I paid only for the tea, and she again refused money for the cakes.

Mr Clifton saw a smart speedboat atop a trailer being reversed over the sands. "He's *not* launching today, surely," Mr Clifton gasped in disbelief.

Wrapped in my lifeguard's heavy red-and-cream canvas jerkin, I sprinted down, shouting. The owner stopped and a familiar conversation took place. "Sorry, you can't launch today; it's too dangerous."

"You can't stop me, pal." He clearly knew lifeguards had no legal power in those days; fortunately, that would all change in the future.

"I can't stop you, but I'll record your demise in my logbook, and please don't pollute our beach with your broken fuel tank."

He gave a small, tolerant smile. "Look, we're just going out for a quick blast; it's my new boat."

"We?" I looked in; he had a small lad beside him, eight or nine years old.

Now I was angry. "Look, please don't launch; didn't you check the forecast? The surf will knock you back anyway and your son will be in great danger. I'm advising you as an expert to an adult. Please."

"Huh, that's it then, we're off." He sped up the small slipway in a spurt of sand, driving in anger. Phew, that was a relief. Returning to the café and half a crossword later, we spotted his boat speeding out from the cove's wee harbour, heading across the bay. He had apparently tried to launch there; again, he'd been warned by the fishermen, several of whom were lifeboatmen, too. He'd rudely ignored them and determinedly launched anyway.

From the café, we spotted his boat skipping over the wind-strewn waves. I watched with dismay through the binocs. "Jesus Christ, his son's aboard too."

Mr Clifton grabbed the binocs. "Will he be OK?" he gasped.

"If he tries to come onto the beach, he'll be pitchpoled by these waves. If he tries to return to the harbour, he'd better make it soon as the dropping tide will see waves breaking across the harbour entrance too."

"What about launching the lifeboat?"

"I may need to call them, but they won't wish to get near this surf break, no cox'n will."

The speedboat had stopped; they seemed to be eating sandwiches and spilling tea, unaware the danger was mounting; the tide was still dropping, and the swell had increased, exactly as forecast, however the sun had come out.

"Oh no, that'll tempt him to come onto the beach," I worried.

Sure as eggs is broken eggs, that's what he tried, approaching the surf break. Telling Mrs Clifton to call the Coastguard 999 if our situation got worse, myself and Mr Clifton, a man in his sixties, were both running down the beach.

The speedboat performed what I described in my logbook as 'two forward somersaults', pitchpoling violently, then resurfacing *sans passagers*, pitchpoling again and resurfacing a second time *sans moteur*. The owner staggered in chest-deep water, coughing, unable to stand, his son floating across the beach on a violent rip. Mr Clifton had clearly been a man of action in his youth; he pointed one hand at the owner the other hand at the son. We naturally split and I waded in to intercept the young boy, putting my float round him and dragging him in to the beach. Mr Clifton had headed for the owner, who was now stumbling and staggering in the inner surf, helping him ashore while swearing loudly in unfamiliar terms. "You bloody, bloody, bloody idiot, you could've killed that lad." He vibrated with rage.

Having partially recovered, the owner looked at his washed-up, damaged boat, checked his keys and said, "Hey, my motor's gone."

"If I find it when the tide's fully out, it'll go in the council tip. Take heed of stormy weather, Captain." I grinned. He squelched off, helping his dripping son.

Mr Clifton and I dripped silently up the beach, our silence saying, *that could have gone very badly indeed.* Later, dry and becoming warm, I headed back to the café to note the details in my logbook over a reheated tea. "That man's a danger," said Mrs Clifton. "You saved the child today but perhaps he's doomed in future by the idiot care of his father."

"He even made Mr Clifton swear," I said unwisely with a giggle. She refused to believe me, taking it as an exaggeration. Later, Derek also refused to believe me. I decided they were right, and I was wrong; Mr Clifton had not sworn; in fact, he had never, ever sworn; the world seemed a much better place that way.

Some days after that episode, I became very ill, with swollen, spongy, bleeding gums and some loose teeth. Classic symptoms of incipient scurvy, I would later discover, but luckily without the bulging eyes, so far, anyway. I biked home to St Ives, where Mother showed much concern but Bungey laughed, diagnosed 'scurvy', sucked his pipe and poured himself a celebratory drink. "Seen it afore!" he announced.

Rising from my sick bed, I visited the doctor. "Scurvy," he diagnosed and queried my dietary habits.

"Pasties, beer, packet-muesli and some mackerel and potatoes," I mumbled defensively through mobile teeth.

"Vitamin C, eat fruit and vegetables; scurvy's common 'round here for undernourished hippies." He waved a prescription note in my face. "Don't try it again or you'll lose all your teeth, sailor. Take these ascorbic acid tablets and you'll be right," he laughed.

I nodded humbly, muttered, "Thank you, Doctor," and scuttled off. Such humiliation, an ancient illness, easily avoided, and my ultimate shame was Bungey diagnosing it immediately. Little did I know it had caused a weakness that would attack my gums again, thirty years afterwards. Solution? Slice gums, polish teeth as deeply as possible, stitch up, repeat for eight dental visits and then I'd be better.

The following afternoon, the council called. As I'd closed the beach, could I pick up some new kit before 5pm? Yes, I could, Penzance here I come; this was my opportunity to visit the library. As I approached town, I thought back to a previous visit to Penzance for supplies. There was a dangerous farm dog which liked to run out, barking frantically. Driving past slowly was out of the question as I had to mount a steep hill just after, so at full throttle, I sped past the farm at about 60mph. The farm dog appeared on cue, barking wildly, misjudged its approach and disappeared, trapped under my bike's fairing. It was now temporarily the fastest dog on earth. I slowed in sympathy; the dog shot out at high speed, hot paws and yowling, jumped over the drystane dyke and never was seen on the road again. Occasionally, yowling would be heard at the sound and oily smell of my passing bike.

Despite my questions during the past few days, no one had produced an answer to 'Kenny's optical confusion'. I suppose I was the one who had time to look and reflect whereas fishermen are busy with their pots and lines, farmers too. With the council's new kit now stacked on my bike, I parked and then beetled into the library, fifteen minutes in hand. Big encyclopaedias are heavy books and time was becoming short. I searched under 'optical illusions' until I found… *'The illusion 'Fata Morgana' in the UK is mainly seen during spring and early summer.*

"Background: an Italian term named after the Arthurian sorceress Morgan le Fay from a belief that these mirages were fairy castles in the air or false land created by her witchcraft to lure sailors to their deaths."

"Listed factors: warm air over a cold sea, temperature inversion giving an atmospheric duct, distortions, shimmering, images rising to double height, inverted or stretched lighthouses."

Perhaps this was the origins of a well-known local legend, recounted as: '*On a clear moonlit night, long ago in the forgotten mists of time, a sailing ship appeared close to the coast between Land's End and Penzance. It came closer and closer to the coast, until everyone believed it would crash onto the rocks. But no! The ship continued to sail over the land until it finally faded from view close to Porthcurno*'. Legends usually have a basis in observation. Hmmm…

The trip back to Sennen had me thinking. Could these 'Fata Morgana' be the legend of Lyonesse (of King Arthur fame?). Lyonesse, the land that disappeared and occasionally reappeared, was believed to lie somewhere beneath the waters that once stretched from the Isles of Scilly to the Cornish shores. When this fabled land was suddenly flooded more than a thousand years ago, only one man, Trevilian, escaped on his white horse. The coat of arms of that family still show a horse rising from the sea.

I saw Derek. "Hey Derek, I found the answer to that mirage."

"Good," he said. "Fishing tomorrow, mackerel again, seven o'clock sharp with the tide or I'll be off without ee."

"Not interested in my mirage, Derek? Ah well, I'm sure at least Captain Summerbee will be interested."

"Ee's like you, boy. Bothers with things that don't turn a profit." Derek smiled slyly, hoping to provoke me, his favourite sport.

"Yes, fishing tomorrow." I conceded victory to Derek's immovable, conscious indifference and dragged my new kit over the sands.

Derek considered me an intellectual, but it was clear to me that I was already on course to fail my maths course, even though only one year had passed. What could I do? My natural ability had deserted me; my original interest in maths had drained away to be replaced by motorbikes, girls, and lifeguarding. Was I worried? Hmmm, I couldn't even decide that. Only in February, after five months at uni, my maths tutor passed me on the stairs, stopped and, with teacherly sarcasm, asked, "Don't I know you?"

Embarrassed, I replied, "Regrettably, yes, you do. That's regrettably for you. I'm sorry, I'll try and 'pull up my britches' or should I say 'baggies.'" I had, predictably, overstated my ambition and slouched on down the stairs, further down the academic scale, as he ascended airily to his deserved dreaming spire.

My money-making continued its erratic path. Some pals in St Ives made surfboards, shaping the foam, fibreglassing it and cleverly painting arresting images before the final gel coat. The effect was stylish and effective for surfing. Cool dudes had custom-made boards. My goal was different; I started by making basic, ugly boards in Derek's shed and he would rent them out from the café to visitors. My board-making was dreadful but hugely profitable for Derek as the boards were almost indestructible. I was so ashamed of my barge-like attempts that I stopped, but Derek urged me on again. "More boards, we're makin' good money, boy, be rich dreckly." He was right about the money but not about the 'we'.

Strong, weightlifting Brummies, pale and tattooed in string vests, would queue up for a chance to impress their girlfriends. For me, the good thing was they couldn't get out past the surf break, thus never needing rescue, just some elementary first aid to pacify their girlfriends. "Look 'e's nor dying, but 'e needs sumat on 'is 'ead, love," they'd say. I'd oblige with a smile. Unfortunately for these guys, surfing requires practice and skill, not muscle and determination. It's the practice and skill that build muscle, not the other way round. Their first session over, covered in blood and spitting teeth, they would return their board with a dribbling, 'Tara-a-bit, see yer temorrer, like' and limp off, telling the world they'd had great fun and only real men like themselves can surf.

Loud the wind howls, loud the waves roar
Thunderclaps rend the air.
'THE SKYE BOAT SONG'.

The loudspeaker relayed the phone's ring. The Coastguard was calling: could I reach two anglers under the cliffs further up the coast before the helicopter arrives? In a direct line, it was two miles, which would take one hour running on a cliff path with no equipment and leaving the beach unattended. "Regretfully, not possible."

Through the binocs, I could just make out one man on the rocks below the cliffs, two miles away to the north, past Nanquidno, a place where piskies can lead mortals far astray. Heavy swells were passing over the rocks and this mortal was clinging on, wet and probably weaker with each passing wave set. I could discern the other man had scrambled up and had run to alert the coastguard, no mobile phones in those days. I saw a knot of onlookers anxiously watching from the cliff area and calculated: ten minutes to reach a phone, ten to scramble the heli-crew, fifteen to transit, so thirty-five minutes total before the chopper arrives. Spring tides come in quickly, e.g, six metres, in six hours, but the tide mounts much faster around the half-tide mark, so I reckoned it had already mounted another metre. The angler would be heavy, bulkily clad, in waders, ideal for drowning.

The helicopter from Royal Naval Air Station (RNAS) Culdrose, a Sikorsky S61, appeared a bit to the east; the onlookers cheered and waved; the heli sped onwards, descending, manoeuvred itself into position, buffeted from the gusts roiling off the cliffs, the waves washing the victim's isolated rock. The angler was being knocked off and dragged back by the waves, then scrambling upwards again. The winchman descended, being dangled and swaying in the wind, raised up again as another wave rolled over the rock. The timing of the pick-up would be critical, I feared, between sets of waves. Silent, now-horrified watchers, their pleasant holiday interrupted by drama and death, the angler's anxious mate, me watching through binocs, we all looked on, breath bated. I had one eye on my beach, where people only paddled; I'd closed it to swimmers. Some competent surfers were braving the breakers.

The winchman inched downwards, the angler clutching skywards as he tried to avoid the waves again. The heli-blades were close to the cliff, but the noise was carried away by the wind, making this a silent drama. The winchman dropped with his straps, expertly attached the angler, checked again, signalled up, and they gracefully ascended, legs cycling as the winch cable turned. They disappeared inside as the helicopter, already with power on, tilted forwards away from the cliffs, then rose, turning towards RNAS Culdrose.

Excitement over, I realised that this was my ambition: all the excitement of military flying, but heli-rescues saved lives instead of ending them, so it's air-sea rescue for me! People sometimes ask themselves, what is their nicest sound: birdsong? Singing? Music? I can tell them it's the sound of an approaching helicopter when a life is in danger.

Lifesavers St. Ives, underfed Kenny, under flagpole. Great guys, my heroes, 1965

Early morning, very early season, Whitesands Bay, Sennen, 1969

Bushy, bushy, bohemian and his board, 1970

Above:
'The Round House', Sennen Cove's winching shed, now a gift shop.

Below:
The Old Success Inn, lounge bar, public bar, drinking car-park, and historic smuggling.

Above:
Sennen's tiny harbour,
looking away to Cape
Cornwall and the
Brisons.

Left:
Mother's best-in-class,
portrait of Kenny. For
God's sake, don't smile.
1970

Above:
"Let's Go Surfin'." (behind Sandy is Mike in the hut) 1972

Below:
"Let's go fishing 6am, tomorrow, a tenner for you and a few mackerel, boy"

Right:
Beauty on the farm,
1972 (Hazel, name has
been changed)

Above:
Maths lecturer puzzles
over his own notes. I,
too, was often puzzled.
1972

Above:
University 'stoodent', Dave, organizing his Roadster, beside my bike, a Triumph 350, 1972

Below:
Beauty in the hippie years

My Triumph Roadster built 1946, rebuilt 1972, graceful, five seats, well-ventilated

Dave drops Dook, I'll be his temporary guardian, 1972

Believe it or not, I'm musically preparing for 1973, my year in America. Photo December 1972.

7

Autumn 1970

Dead Man's Curve...

Ignorance is the parent of fear.
HERMAN MELVILLE, *MOBY DICK.*

ick and I met up at Penzance's Union pub, with the girls on pillion, and drove to the White Lion pub, fondly nicknamed 'The Groin Exchange'. 'Twas a dark, wet evening, and in the courtyard, there was a blocked fountain with floating lilies. In an uncharacteristically helpful mood, I tried to unblock the fountain's nozzle by stepping forwards onto the lilies, thinking it very shallow, but I'd stepped into three feet of water. I didn't know that lilies floated on deep water, thus, soaked to the skin, I managed to half dry off over two pints beside a roaring fire. Then, we set off for Zennor Arms, riding through Ding Dong (Cornish *ding*, meaning 'dell'), a strange place as nobody has found it since 1877 when the mine closed. The copper mine was rumoured to have been the source of the copper for King Solomon's temple three thousand years ago. The road sign says 'Ding Dong ½ mile', so you drive the half mile, nothing, continue on until reaching a sign pointing back the way you've just come, 'Ding Dong ½ mile'. Repeat the exercise, then again, nothing. Asking farming locals, you find that there indeed once was a village with a mine, a mill and even a chapel. The remaining vestige is the Ding Dong Bell at nearby Madron. That's Cornwall, folks, signposts to nowhere.

Reaching the Zennor Arms, a couple more pints, then we set off home, the night still dark and wet hawthorns scratching at our helmets. We weren't drunk by local standards, so we set off along the B3306 into a typical Cornish night of scudding gloom along a road with no catseyes. We knew it well enough during the day, but difficulties descended with the night: swaying trees, gusts of rain and the surface lit weakly by our weak motorbike lights. I followed Mick's red tail light, occasionally seeing his headlight partly illuminating the winding granite 'hedges' ahead. West Cornwall 'hedges' were dangerous as sometimes they're only thinly veneered by greenery, but behind are solid granite lumps punctuated by an occasional, broken, five-bar gate. We sped along, warmed slightly by our engines and the reassuring hugging of our pillion 'blondes', who in my case was a brunette. Trying to make out the black road on a black night, I thought, *Mick's a bit fast*, approaching what we would later call 'Dead Man's Curve'. He didn't even try to take the curve. From my view, he had just disappeared. Miraculously, he had traversed where there was a gap in the granite, no bike, no Mick, no girlfriend, no tail light. I was also going faster than wise but made the curve in a state of shock, braking carefully, anxious to help Mick, 'blonde' and bike. Then, in my mirror, I saw his headlight re-emerge, now behind me, bumping back onto the road, his bike festooned with branches. Awakened birds sprayed in all directions. We both stopped. He'd gone through the vegetation, traversed a murky pool and several gnarled trees, re-emerging back on the road. We disentangled the branches and checked both Mick and 'blonde' were unhurt, apart from some scratches and shock. Mick complained of his jaw where a stout branch had ridden over his fairing, bent under sudden tension, then whiplashed his face. Some blood, not much, we laughed. Tough-guy Mick shook his head and we all carried on, parting at the tiny St Just grass airstrip, us to Sennen, them to Porthcurno.

I called the following morning, his parents saying that Mick was at the doctors complaining about his jaw. I popped over later to find him repairing his damaged fairing. He was still in pain, but the doc had pronounced him bruised, stirred *and* shaken but not damaged. Forsaking his painkillers, he carried on fixing his bike. The next day, he was back at the doctor, who insisted he actually ingest the painkillers. "They are more efficient when out of the bottle, dear boy."

At parental insistence, on day three, he ignored the doctor and visited the dentist. "My boy, you've broken your finely chiselled jaw." So that was that; both Mick and his fairing became well wired up.

I called to see him; he mumbled his news, "Got something important to tell you."

"What?"

"We're emigrating, Marion and I together."

"Where to?" I said, shocked, wondering silently who could leave West Cornwall, especially before securing a decent education?

"To Australia, as ten pound poms."

"To Oz? But you can't!"

"Why not?"

"Because I'm the surfer; it's surfers who are supposed to emigrate to Oz! You're a squash player. You should emigrate to Pakistan, India, or Egypt and play more squash."

We laughed, but I was very upset. Our close lives, bikes, lifeguarding, girls, plus being great friends, all to be lost. Mick realised how upset I was and quietly explained they wouldn't leave until next autumn, by which time their application should be approved, but they already met the main criterion: they were white. This was 1970 and the Australian Government's whites-only policy, whilst no longer official, was still in effect. Now they were saving and planning to sell their possessions before departure.

I knew the term 'ten pound pom'. For £10, a family could get a ship's passage to Australia, taking three weeks via the Cape. Tickets and meals were all included, plus an apartment in, say, Adelaide, for six months, and introductory jobs. Two youngsters, able, energetic, probably fertile, just what a growing country needed. The normal price would have been £300 at £150 per head.

Mick and I were undoubtedly best friends. In the various towns my family had lived, I'd never liked groups of boys, hating the very idea of gangs, but I usually had one very good friend, and now this friend was planning to leave. With our girlfriends, we had been a 'gang of four', happy together. My crest had now truly fallen. My father had died when I was an infant; we then moved from Fairlie to Ardrossan; our mother had remarried; then we moved down to St Ives, in Cornwall. Then, my stepfather had died and we moved to Lelant. Mother had remarried again, so stepfather number two – Bungey, a retired sea captain – entered our lives. My eldest sibling, sister Sheila, had recently qualified as a doctor and had emigrated to Barbados in 1968. Now, my best chum was heading off. To a young lad, it was so unfair with everyone leaving. In my imagination, it was me who was supposed to leave them, with just a 'hey-ho and a hey-nonny no' and ne'er a backwards glance. Their role was to stay put, grieve my departure and pine for me forever, not the other way round. I'd show them all, I decided several times; I'd go to the USA and trump everyone. Ooo-er, that may clash with my flying ambitions, plus the small matter of uni.

After summer, Helen came to uni with me. We stayed in a damp flat in the prostitutes' area of St Mary's Road. The city of Southampton was a major port and prostitutes were in high demand. Housing standards were ignored, so our flat had water seeping behind the wallpaper and bulging out until pricked and drained. Sailors and pros filled the other flats above, and we stayed damp in our basement, with only my motorbike and Helen's mynah bird for company. Helen was a wonderful person; she cooked, cleaned and found a job at the Ford factory nearby. She had a classy, hippy look, wore floral prints, had floaty, long, jet-black hair and, when out walking, she was never bothered by sailors. She was clearly far too beautiful to be 'on the game'. In fact, people in the street stared in disbelief. Luckily, this flat was only for autumn term, however whilst we were still living in St Mary's Road, my brother Eoin would, true to form, disrupt our settled life.

Luckily, I'd recently bought a Morris Traveller with a wooden body frame; in the USA it would be called a 'woodie'. Jan and Dean even dedicated a song to their woodie in Surf City. Mine served as a car, a van for transporting bits for friends and a campervan with a mattress in the rear. Perfect for a surfer and his trips from Southampton down to Cornwall.

This Traveller would soon be useful. Brother Eoin, with his new wife, Maggie, and baby Oonagh, would emigrate this winter to Oz. Living in Glasgow, Eoin was nine years older than me, notoriously clandestine, never flagging his movements in advance, this time with good reason as he was avoiding some 'Glasgie hard men' who expected their money back. Eoin called me, out of the blue. "Kenneth, it's your beloved brother Eoin, we're emigrating, but don't tell anyone."

"What do you mean 'we', Kemo Sabe?" said I, recovering quickly and using the old Lone Ranger joke.

"Maggie, Oonagh and me, that's who we is," he whispered urgently with confusing grammar through the background bustle of a busy railway station.

"Well, when? Why call me at nine o'clock at night to tell me this?"

"Because we're changing trains here at Birmingham and arriving in Southampton on the train at half past ten tonight. Can you put us up? We're departing from the dock at eleven o'clock in the morning!"

"Gosh, errr, yes, but no food here and just bedding on the floor. What about baby?"

"We have everything for baby. Don't worry. Can you pick us up at the station at half past ten, we sleep over, and then you drive us to the dock tomorrow morning? Getting to the dock for nine o'clock latest."

"Errrr, yes, if the van starts OK, it's freezing here."

"OK, see you at the station; our train's on time and leaving in two minutes." Click.

The already-short night passed quickly while Eoin and I, over the residue of a bottle of whisky, discussed their 'sudden' future. Eoin, fast becoming maudlin, reached over, spilling his whisky.

And there's a hand, my trusty fiere
And gie's a hand o' thine
And we'll tak a right gude willy-waught
For auld lang syne.

ROBERT BURNS, 'AULD LANG SYNE'

We both shook and wept while Maggie and Oonagh slept, squeezed into the single bed beside Helen. Eoin and I had been relegated to the floor.

"£10?" I gasped in the dark. "If I'd known it was so cheap, I'd have sent you years ago," I joked, sadly shaking my head and turning away to hide my tears.

In the morning, we all awoke from the cold and damp. Eoin and I bump-started the 'woodie' down the incline, scraped the windscreen, loaded everyone and suitcases and set off into Southampton's morning traffic, waving to Helen who was still startled from this unheralded turn of events. Eoin's explanation for emigrating was opaque, however they'd kept everything close to their chests, and after six months of 'finessed' paperwork, they were setting off to Adelaide, aboard the *SS Arcadia* as ten pound poms, costing just £10 assisted passage for the whole family, three weeks aboard, all meals, sunbeds, deck quoits and a coaling stop at the Cape of Good Hope.

The word 'pom' is derived from 'pomegranate', an Australian rhyming slang for 'immigrant' which, bizarrely, doesn't rhyme very well. In Eoin's case, I preferred the alternative sobriquet, POM: Prisoner Of Her Majesty. Following the twenty-three signs to the berth, we drove into Southampton dock as the earlier emigrants were boarding via the gangways. Swiftly, Eoin was checking in their suitcases, a quick hug to me, and they were boarding with the others.

"There have been more auspicious departures," I said, pointing to a brass plaque:

In memory of the passengers and crew of the RMS Titanic which sailed from the nearby Berth 43 on her maiden voyage on 10th April 1912 and sank on 15th April 1912 with the loss of over 1500 lives.

I was hung over, short of sleep, stunned at these sudden events, and now there they were, gone. They mounted the steep gangway holding the handrails; I stood back amongst the other relatives, not·wishing to inadvertently go to Australia. The ships' railings thronged with passengers, mainly young people setting sail for their new lives. As the cables were dropped, all the emigrants were given ribbons to throw to their loved ones on the quayside. These ribbons streamed down and, as the ship departed, they broke; there was more public weeping than the Wailing Wall, a lifetime of love ruptured by a damp ribbon. Head cast down, I walked away and wept in my 'woodie'. Fare thee well, dear brother, you are leaving today and Best Pal Mick will leave next year. So much sadness, but my cheery little childhood-self had always known that Lady Serendipity, plus a little adventuring, shall provide this undeserving wretch with a satisfactory future. I'll see them again, I swore.

Spring term came and Dave's dad had provided a spare caravan. Dave would bring it on a low-loader to Winchester, near uni, put it on a farm beside the horse stables and his residents would be Dave himself, Richard, me, Helen and two fascinating birds, plus occasional rats attracted by the birds: Dave's sulphur-crested cockatoo, Dook, and Helen's greater Indian hill mynah, topically named Woodstock. In a snowy mid-January '71, we all moved into the warmth of our caravan. Dave was constantly puzzled by my relationship with Helen. How come I can help anyone and everyone with bikes, gardens, fixing things but still treat Helen badly? I was puzzled as I was always affectionate to her, sorted her money worries and still Dave seemed to criticise me. I must be unfeeling, apparently, expecting Helen to follow me to uni, back to Sennen, then off to uni again. Maybe I've always been this way. Not my opinion but in the opinion of my friends, Dave and Richard.

Triumph Roadster 2000, rebuilding in the snow, instead of studying, 1971

That spring in Southampton, I'd pursue an obsession to distract me from maths: a Triumph Roadster 2000. A car old before her time, built just after WWII, a touring convertible with a three-speed, column gear change, her bonnet the length of a canal boat, giving enough space to have three front seats, each with its own windscreen wiper. She looked like a sports car but was much bigger, having two 'dicky seats' in the boot. Passengers merely opened the boot, pulled out these two seats, raised the second windscreen and stepped in via the rear bumper, so five seats in all. I bought her as a write-off that had recently destroyed a London taxi on the North Circular and thus had damaged her wings and big, chrome headlamps. Cheap at £50, full of character and of robust build. Could I restore her to action? You bet! The steel chassis was indestructible; the body was aluminium on an ashwood frame; the wings could be knocked out into a pleasing shape; the hood could be replaced; and the running parts were mainly Land Rover, thus easily obtainable. My motivation was to avoid studying, so I'd just found a reason to distract myself. Many hours of work, in the freezing conditions of this Southampton winter, brought her to driving order. Years later, this model of car would feature in ten years of the TV crime series *Bergerac*, set in Jersey. I had her ready for March, and with Helen, we enjoyed the springtime, blasting hood down through the New Forest and surrounds, before just scraping my end-of-year exams.

Maths lecturer puzzles over his own notes. I, too, was often puzzled, 1972

I could arrive 'triumphantly' into Sennen Cove ready for the summer of '71, only a year before the much-wished end of uni. My arrival into Sennen was enhanced because Dave had entrusted me with his bird, Dook. Dook was a big, sulphur-crested cockatoo with a crippled foot, named Duke but pronounced Dook. Dook had been entrusted to me as he already knew me well and would 'behave' during the summer. With the hood down and the wind in his feathers, Dook would ride on the top of the windscreen, bobbing up and down, at speeds up to 30mph, crest extended, cawing hoarsely, distracting other drivers and puzzling police officers who were sure we were breaking the law, if only they could find a relevant offence.

I recalled the library book describing how to care for these striking, intelligent birds:

'Cockatoos do not thrive on birdseed alone', so hang on, Dook!

8

Summer 1971

And Echoes in the Mists of Silence

How it stands there, away off shore,
more lonely than the Eddystone lighthouse.
HERMAN MELVILLE, *MOBY DICK*

Is it possible to be awoken by silence? An eerie silence with thick fog lurked outside with its dampness invading my blankets. Not a sound of wind or waves, not a voice, not a gull even, as the gulls' chief pilot had probably cancelled flying on this foggy day. Just total silence. Could silence alone have awakened me?

Then, I heard a sound from my happy childhood on the Ayrshire coast, a short, even drone, a lowing like a cow from the high pastures of Asgard, dwelling place of the Norse gods. In Ayrshire, we all heard the signature moans of Ailsa Craig and Pladda lighthouses as they lowed their mellifluidity on low-visibility days; ships bound for Glasgow sounded their own foghorns, feeble by comparison. A lighthouse's foghorns were majestic, travelling twenty-five miles to mariners' ears. The keepers, close to the foghorns but fortunately behind them, must have been driven crazy with such a repetition lasting several days during those high-pressure, foggy periods. Each foghorn's identifying period was different, so it seemed that they were replying, a conversation of mythical beings. I carefully uncovered Dook's cage; he was still asleep, head tucked behind in his feathers. Cockatoos are actively intelligent, social birds. He needed at least ten hours of shut-eye and could be particularly stroppy if he didn't get his beaky sleep.

Another lonesome, mournful bass droned across the misty bay. "Fnooonnnngggg!" The signature sound of the nearby Longships Lighthouse was a coded blast every ten seconds. "Fnooonnnngggg!" with a ten-second gap, thus a mariner peering through the damp gloom could be sure it was indeed Longships, prior to ironically going aground on the very skerry sounding the warning. As I listened to the soothing bellows, I scribbled on a piece of paper: distance to Longships was two and a half miles, speed of sound at sea level 1,100 feet/sec, thus the signal took twelve seconds to reach my beach. My A-level physics reminded me the reason a foghorn's frequency was so low. It's because sounds with lower pitches have a longer wavelength, meaning the sound wave can cover a greater distance and easily pass around barriers like rocks. This property of a wave signal is called diffraction… the longer the sound wave's length, the easier it is for the wave to do this and, because long wavelengths scrape the sea less times, their attenuation is reduced and could be heard up to twenty-five miles away in poor visibility. Enough physics!

In Britain, the last foghorns would sound their expiring breath in about 1985, but in Sumburgh in Shetland, a restoration by dedicated engineers now means this beautiful sound can still be enjoyed on special occasions. Childhood can be revived and reverberations appreciated anew.

Peering out the window into blank nothingness, I thought, *great, a relaxed day with no one around, catch up on my reading*, then a worrying thought came, *how do I know there isn't some fool willing to go swimming today?* I planned to patrol the shoreline every forty-five minutes, timing my megaphone warnings between blasts.

"Fnooonnnngggg!" Lasting ten seconds.

"Beware, beware, any swimmers cannot—"

"Fnooonnnngggg!" Lasting ten seconds.

"… be seen by the lifeguard."

"Fnooonnnngggg!" Lasting ten seconds. "Fnooonnnngggg!" again.

Checking my watch, I started out and reached the beach café fifteen minutes later. Mrs Clifton saw me emerge from the dense fog, still swirling but lifting slowly. "This is the noisiest day of my life," she laughed. "The foghorn and your megaphone!"

"Wait till I finish rebuilding my bike engine and set off up the hill."

"Are you finishing it soon?"

"Just awaiting the piston rings, praying they are the correct size, and putting everything back together. Will Derek help me carry the engine back across the beach?"

"Only if you pay him." She winked as Derek emerged.

I spoke up, "His reward will come in Heaven, if he ever gets there, probably by a clerical error on the part of St Peter."

"Ha, ha," said Derek. "'Ere, boy, fancy a tenner 'elpin' wi' a seal?" He sucked his teeth and tilted his head. Sure enough, behind the rocks, there was a dead seal thirty yards from the café. "Wot're ee doing tomorrow evenin', boy?"

"Probably beating you at skittles in the Old Success, if there's no decent surf, I suppose."

"'Ere, boy, I thought you stoodent wasters was supposed to be intellectuals," complained Derek.

"We are, but fun and gallivanting come first, Derek, especially with a large student grant to fritter away on beer and skittles," I mocked.

"Zackly, that's what my mum says – she says you're doing more than your fair share of gallivanting. And my sister, she knows your sister, like."

I sighed my usual exasperation at this 'your business is everybody's business' attitude. "For a man in your twenties, Derek, you have an unhealthy interest in my apparently unsecret social life."

"Well, you've a lot to be secret about. I'm 'ere working all day, no chance for a romantic life, me, not like you stoodents."

"Yes, Derek, but unlike me, you'll be a millionaire, you Cliftons are already land owners, café owners and I hear you're now becoming a contractor to the council."

"'at's what I wants to talk about. Do ee smell that stink, boy?"

I sniffed the air. Yes, I did smell it, rotting flesh, not too strong. "You should clean that ice-cream machine more often, Derek."

"Cheeky bugger, you are. Anyway, a dead seal was washed ashore at high tide last night, smelt it this mornin' an' covered it with that piece o' tarpaulin, see?"

I looked to where he pointed over near the rocks on the left. Sure enough, a black tarp poked out from some sand Derek had shovelled over. "Are you planning to move it?"

"Yes, soon as the council agrees to up the price."

"They might send some workmen immediately; after all, it is a health hazard."

"Too busy, they are, peak season, see, an' weekend's comin', so they'll 'ave to pay double time. By Monday, it'll drive people off the beach."

"Yes, but you're the beach owner and so you'd stand to lose custom."

"Right there, boy, but it's a, wots-it-called, stand-off now."

"A Mexican stand-off."

"See, you are an intellectual, my cock," he mocked triumphantly.

I felt I'd been tricked again. "Anyway, you only strike up conversations when money's involved," I sneered, knowing his proposition was coming and it had to involve me and a pitiful sum dripped into my ever-ready pocket. "How will we manage this task, boss?"

"I'll tell ee wot, you 'n' me dig a hole, roll the body onto the tarp and slide it up onto the wagon. Weighs about three hundred pounds. Should be OK for two of us with a bit of rolling." Derek ducked into his shed to the ringing phone, a brief conversation, and emerged smiling the smile of a capitalist casino owner who holds all the chips and the best cards. "They blinked first, see, gotta do it soonest today, when not many on the beach, 'cept you 'n' me, see? Ready to earn £5?"

I knew he'd chosen me as the lowest cost flexible fool available, who wouldn't say too much. "What are you planning to do with it? Public health dumps cost money."

"Well, I 'ear that these grape vines like a pig or somethin' dug into their roots, does 'em a treat, see? Proper job."

"Aha, so you'll be paid by the council to clean it off, and quickly, paid too to transport it away, and paid by the vine owner, who, I guess, is that slightly famous artist lady with the amazing garden at Pendeen. That means lifting by us at both ends, cos she can't help. Sounds like £15 to me."

"I'll see ee at half past nine tomorrow morning – wear gloves."

"You said you agreed with the council to move it soonest today," I queried.

"They won't know it's bein' done tomorrow," he triumphed. "I'll bring the stuff, and you can expect £12 in cash."

Derek believed that £1 in cash was worth £2 in any other method of legal tender, and for him it was. The famed Cornish wreckers had left a legacy, and I would often be a partial beneficiary. My ability to do anything almost legal that would enrich Derek, preferably at unusual hours, meant I could start saving for travelling.

The high pressure of the foggy days meant no worthwhile surf, so in the empty car park we surfers could entertain ourselves on skateboards.

Skateboarding, or sidewalk surfing, was yet another Californian craze we were all avidly practising. We could swap injuries like surf knots on feet and knees for scrapes and scratches on our heads. "Make the most of this skateboarding, guys!" Like surfing, it's skilful, episodic and hedonistic. I was checking the pressure charts, a big change, looks like heavy surf with onshore winds coming tomorrow afternoon, so I'd need to be on duty smartish after fishing.

Managing a surf beach with big tides can be tricky. Tide in: easy work, I can patrol from the shortened beach, close to the water and keep an eye on everybody, whilst chatting to visitors, dispensing advice and cheery bonhomie. Tide out: the beach is much wider, the water distant, so I had to retreat atop the sand dunes for height, using binocs to observe. It's a long way to run carrying a rescue surfboard, so I'd leave the board near the water, which meant it had to be moved every twenty minutes of tide, and small, sandy children had to be warned off.

Sectioning a beach for a bathing area is an art of understanding changing sandbanks, their rips and undertow, how the waves and wind affect the beach and a divination of how it will all progress in order to avoid continually repositioning my red-and-yellow squared flags. Sometimes, it can be safest where the best surf is, but now there's a problem: to keep the surfers onside and more-or-less obeying the area, as who knows when I may need them. Before ankle straps that keep surfers attached to a loose board when he 'wiped out', the board would become a projectile, spinning and whirling, before being taken sideways towards the paddling public further inside. Make the area too small and the public ignore it; make it too big and I cannot police it all, plus some surfers would self-righteously intrude. Waves belong to surfers only, right? They could take off from outside the bathing area, surf across it, weaving through the swimmers, and exit the area before a wipeout or kickout. Placing the bathing area is a balance as I need the surfers onside to help occasional swimmers in difficulty; they were usually closer than me. I had no pride in this respect; this lifeguard didn't mind who saved a swimmer, provided they were indeed saved. 'It doesn't matter the colour of a cat, provided it catches the mice', a saying later ascribed to Deng Zhou Ping. For any Russian or Chinese quotes, I received highest praise from Communist John as he studied his much-fingered, nicotine-stained Little Red Book. Others just looked baffled.

I'd query John. "Are you really a paid-up member of the Communist Party?"

He'd smile his warmest smile. "No, can't afford it, but it really enrages the county types that read their right-wing rags, like the Daily Express. Careful how you spell 'county' now," he added with a guffaw.

In the early days of lifeguards, there were no bye-laws to give us authority for bathing areas and orders or advice on the beach. Years later, that would change; the professionalism and level of training would be higher and qualifications awarded by the RNLI. Equipment would become astoundingly better, and manpower would increase. I covered a large, busy beach with heavy surf by myself, armed only with a surfboard for rescues. Now it's three persons, a Land Rover and two jet-skis. From the lookout's alert to the casualty is quick, and retrieval is assured. Alone with my surfboard, often I was in fear of losing someone, or being busy when another event was taking place further down the beach.

A common event was an angina event happening. A typical visitor leaves his angina tablets in the B&B (or even forgets to bring them on holiday). He drives the family car to Cornwall on a Friday night, gets up on the Saturday morning, has a full Cornish breakfast, and shepherds his family down to the beach. Invigorated by sun and sea air, he goes for a swim, for him, an unaccustomed exercise. His enthusiasm leads him into the surf; he waves to his family during much excited jumping. However, he's a sensible man and stays within his depth but then –gasp – clutching at his heart, his legs give way as he feels weaker. With legs bent, he's no longer within his depth and begins floundering. His happy family still thinks he's waving but then they become concerned. Usually, I would spot this small knot of mother and two kids looking around for others to help and I would pick up my binocs. Sure enough, it's a rescue! I'm already running down the beach, others are entering the water to try and reach him. A human almost floats when he's in a swimming pool but he's a heavy load in the surf, which is half foam, and he's wetly slippery. The others can't hold him, but I'm already there, pushing my surfboard underneath him. We hoist him on and carry him through the gathering onlookers, using the surfboard now as a stretcher. We make him comfortable. Sometimes, a paramedic or doctor appears, giving me a chance to quiz the victim's wife.

She says, "Ee's got stable angina, but all 'is tablets is at our B&B ten miles away an' I can't drive."

I megaphone along the beach for someone with a similar condition and bingo! An elderly gentleman appears, a capsule of similar tablets wisely tucked in his trunks. Ten minutes have passed; the café offers to call for an ambulance, but the gentleman is feeling slightly better and typically wants no fuss.

"This feller 'ere gimme tablets, same as mine, just need a rest, be OK then. Don't want to spoil us 'olidays. Worse fings 'appen at sea, eh?" he says quietly, through a weak smile, as his wife holds his hand, raising her eyes at his attempted humour. I'll take their details later for my logbook. All is now well and time to re-scan the beach for other possible victims volunteering for their own demise. Thus, continues a normal day on a beach.

Derek appeared. "Fishing tomorrow early, big runs coming, boy. Hard work for you and hard cash for me!" That was the closest to a Derek joke as I'd ever heard. He was right, too. The following day, our haul was so great, Derek had to sell it at the fish market in Newlyn. He returned later that morning, "Got paid for a delivery of bricks on the return, too, boy," and paid me my £10 with a flourish. "Want to 'elp me unload, another £5 for you, boy?" Unloading finished, it was still only 10am and Derek produced a bag containing a dozen market oysters. "A present. Got 'em for free at the market. No one'll eat 'em 'round 'ere, see. For you and that pretty girl, boy, reckon you'll need 'em, considerin' the reputation of oysters, an' all." We both laughed. He'd guessed correctly, and I did like oysters.

The following morning, chatting in the car park, I told Derek how much I'd enjoyed those fresh oysters. John was all ears at this strange conversation about oysters.

"You deserves 'em oysters, boy," said Derek.

"True, true, but I have a complaint."

"Woz that then, boy?"

"Only eleven of them worked," I winked.

John laughed aloud at this banter and Derek looked rueful; he must really stop his money chase and make some time to get himself a real girlfriend. He had plenty of opportunity at his ice-cream stall on the beach. Shyness can be disabling for a man, even one as good-looking and moneyed as Derek.

Sometimes, there are days just perfect for surfing. At high tide, surfers can delight in autumn's perfect, warmed waters, the afternoon's lowering sun heating the body, the surf's break very close to the last, steep part of the beach, an offshore wind holding up the wave-front vertically with the low sun glinting through. Spectators love it as they're close to the action and feel almost that they themselves are riding the wave. The surfer catches the wave, jumps up quickly, drops in, a fast base turn, speedy manoeuvres, and with precision timing, kicks out just before the wave crashes noisily onto the steeply shelving, almost-dry pebbles at the watchers' feet. At this point, after a holiday of seeing skilful surfers in the far distance, the spectators realise you can't actually surf a wave unless you really work at all the associated abilities. Surfers see more beauty than most, and it's with you all your life, every moment, no matter where you are and whatever you're doing. The spectators for once see up-close the beauty and power in both the water and the skilful pursuit of the wave. That's the ecstasy of this particular passion; it's difficult, fleeting, dangerous but so satisfying. 'Stoked' is a word that can apply only to surfing. We've been surfing all summer long, but it won't be long till summer's gone; meanwhile, we can bask in the warmth of the sun.

Surf, St. Ives lookout, tube, recent photo

Surfing has taught me a simple truth; we see more beauty than most.
A beauty that's with you every moment, no matter what you're doing.
ELLIS AVERY, AMERICAN WRITER.

9

Autumn 1971

Two Lasses for Every Laddie...

A beauty and power in both the water and pursuit of the wave,
Surfers are surfers for all time.

ELLIS AVERY, AMERICAN WRITER.

Coming down my sand dune, I see Sandy walking her two dogs. "Kenny, ee knows Trevor, don' ee?"

"I do. We hitch-hiked recklessly to Scotland together one summer five years ago; I was thirteen; he was fourteen. You must have heard about that disaster."

"Well, no one talks 'bout thaat, see. Anyways, ees gettin' married soon."

"Trevor? He's just one year older than me; we've both just left school. Who's he marrying?"

"Derek's sister and soon, too."

"Wow, good choice! I approve of his selection but not his timing in life. Anyway, I thought cove-ers traditionally didn't marry villagers. In St Ives, the 'Upalongers' traditionally don't marry 'Downalongers' and even have slightly different accents."

"Well, 'ceptions can be made, like in this case. Clifton's got a good name 'ere, village and cove."

"I wish them both well."

"I'll pass on your message cos tidn't likely you'll be invited." Sandy was referring to that notorious hitch-hike trip to Scotland in '64. Setting off from Cornwall, Trevor and I reached Scotland quite quickly in three days, via Manchester to visit his uncle, and then hitching further north, staying at YMCAs. Lucky with the weather, we climbed Ben Nevis. On reaching the top, we had a blazing row, about a topic long-since forgotten, and descended separately, swearing, and swearing never to talk again.

We hitched separately back to Cornwall; I arrived a day before Trevor, and I was in big trouble with his mother. "You just abandoned him? Where is he?" she howled with justified hysteria.

"I didn't abandon him. He's older than me. We just fell out."

"Fell out?" she screamed as only a distraught mother can. She contacted the police, who asked her where Trevor might be. "Probably somewheres 'tween the top of Ben Nevis an' Land's End."

"Madame, that's most of the country horizontally and all of it vertically. We can only record Trevor as 'missing' and then keep looking. Call us immediately if he turns up."

Trevor arrived a day later quite pleased with himself, but the blame still stuck to me.

I considered explaining my version of this to Sandy, who would already know anyway, but as an outsider, I would always be clearly to blame: "Wish them both well in marriage and advise them not to argue on top of Ben Nevis." That was perhaps a mean remark, but 'never apologise, never explain' was my maxim in Sennen. Sandy turned to her dogs, and they set off; had I just lost another friend?

Most mornings, I'd walk over to the toilets in the car park. Leaving the calm of my morning sand dune, I'd be astonished at the frenetic scene of increasing mayhem as cars queued to enter, blocking the road along to the cove. Attendant John, the Liverpudlian communist and avowed, cheerful philosopher, would stomp around waving his crooked fingers, his arthritic digits giving an air of added authority. John's goal was to maximise the cars, which meant added income for the council, and this meant selecting variously sized cars from the queue and bringing them forwards, slotting them in according to his efficient plan, which in consequence meant a modest bonus from the council. A cheery wave from John, but no conversation until he had established a pleasing pattern and reached his maximum, so I'd be back for a chat after my toilet visit. I came out as John was chastising dog owners. "Take the dog with you – he'll fry in the car."

"We'll come back every half hour."

"If you're leaving him, you'll need two windows open and his water bowls filled up."

"Sorry, attendant, we don't have any bowls. He'll be OK."

"No, he won't, no dog or child can survive hours in a sun-drenched car, so take him with you."

The battle would continue as sensible John's experienced advice would be politely dismissed as the ramblings of a long-haired, bearded, troll. Both John and I knew that come 11am, neglected dogs would be howling and later just panting weakly; John would be passing me car registrations and I'd be megaphoning along the beach, searching for negligent dog owners. Every summer, dogs would be found suffering from in-car heat exhaustion or even dead by teatime. Our nightmare was sometimes infants, left unseen, while their parents queued for ice cream. It's difficult, but possible, to break a car window. My recommendation is a sharp lump of granite and the application of youthful energy.

I took the opportunity to collar John about his name. "Hey, John, you seem to be the only person around here with a 'normal' name, John. Are you sure it's not Jonah? Biblical, sea, whales…"

"No, I'm just plain, ordinary John, but you might be interested in my surname."

"What's that? Maybe Stalin, Trotsky, Lenin?" I joked.

"No, but you can have three guesses every day. You'll get it eventually."

John was a great source of opinion and advice. He had lived long enough in a deprived part of Liverpool, fought enough in the Far East in WWII and been a union officer, having a clear, loudly expressed political viewpoint. Being partially deaf and unable to hear himself, John's shouted opinions carried the length of the car park; Britain's population needed to 'ditch those effin' Tories before they ruin us', close the private schools, have more free university places for the working class and invest in British industry before 'them Japs and their effin' motorbikes eat our effin' dinner'. A warm, humorous man, he well recognised that he seemed odd to others in a repressed Britain, and he didn't care. I was his sympathetic ear, but his shouting could only be endured at a distance of several car lengths. He disapproved of Britain's return to Tory rule, and we were all doomed, with the lucky exception of the pill being recently invented. "Bloody great, that pill, wish they 'ad it in my day. Sex was unnatural, according to the Church and Tories. You wanted it; she wanted it, especially the Catholics, who would suffer in Hell, but shame or married were your only options."

"Are you married, John?"

"Was, wack, was, but she died in childbirth, couldn't marry again, just couldn't." John could be loud, sad, liberal, prudish and sentimental all at the same time. He distracted himself by picking up a newspaper; he was obsessive about car park tidiness and also read all the papers, especially to mock the 'Tory rags'. Free newspapers were the only perk of his job, and he would pore over them, issuing hoots of laughter and gnashes of teeth, finishing with great relish, screwing a 'Tory rag' into the bins.

Many people still had jobs that were given to those with war wounds or disablement. For his job, John was torn between gratitude and rage that 'crumbs from the top table', which were both a benefit and an insult. His rage would last seconds, and his natural, sunny disposition would return again, until he saw litter being dropped. "We live in a beautiful country ruined by readers of 'Tory rags'," he would moan and then wryly laugh, "Bloody emets! Here, Kenny, what's an emet, anyway – I thought they were called grockles down here?"

"They're called both. An emet means an ant and describes the tourists cos they only come in the summer and run away when it rains. Grockles and emets are mocking insults. Like you, for instance, you're an old goat," I informed him kindly.

Smiling at his outpourings, I walked past the café: grockles wrestling with deckchairs blocked the path, renegade children screaming about ice cream – it was still only 10am. Derek, the café owners' son, peered out from his deckchair store. Sucking his teeth again, he mimed a digging action.

"Another seal, maybe tomorrow."

"Hey, Derek, maybe a 'selkie' seal hid its skin when changing into a human for romance. Maybe it'll reclaim its skin and return to the sea," I ventured.

"Only piskies and mermaids 'round 'ere, boy. Anything else gets eaten. Anyways, what's this selkie?"

"Well, Derek, wherever there are seals, on most coastlines there's a legend about them coming ashore and taking up human form. They hide their skin and later, they have a family with a human and, unexpectedly, they find their skin and then always return to their home, the sea. Listen, Derek:

I am a man upon the land, I am a selkie in the sea,
And when I'm far and far from land, my home is in Sule Skerry.

'THE GREAT SELKIE' (TRAD.)

.

"That's what we calls sex with animals, might be all right in Devon but 'tis frowned upon down 'ere, my cock. 'Ave a look at this." Derek pulled back the tarp.

I examined the seal; it was definitely dead, bereft of life, it had expired a few days ago, its eyes pecked out by gulls. The usual pattern for mammals and humans is to die in the water with lungs filling up, sink for three days, develop rot in the gut, swell up and resurface, to float until the tide deposits them on a downcurrent shore.

Looking closely, I said, "Derek, this has been here, out of the water, for more than a couple of days."

Derek smiled his monetary smile. "'ad to wait till she's ripe so the council would agree good money for a quick disposal."

I realised yet again why Derek would stay here and become rich whilst I would roam the world, taking my good fortune where I might find it. "OK, Derek, this afternoon is good, maybe late afternoon if the beach is still busy."

"Four o'clock, fog'll be back – we can work a bit hidden, see, till five o'clock." He sucked his teeth to indicate that all equipment would be supplied, tarpaulin, spades, and Land Rover.

At 4pm, with the fog just lifting and the temperature rising, the sun started burning through. Derek was keen to be unseen. "Dead seals, bad for business! Makes the emets cry." He sucked his teeth mournfully. So, now surrounded by mist and behind the rocks, we dug a hole in the sand, lined it with tarpaulin and readied to roll the carcass in. Adult grey males weigh 250kg and are 10ft in length, needing a sizable hole. The seal had to roll gently inside otherwise it would break open and disintegrate. Sweating, we levered mightily and rolled it in. Yes, it split open as it rolled; we staggered back, coughing and retching, heads spinning, close to vomiting.

Stepping back into clear air so we could breathe, Derek nodded with satisfaction and a suck of his teeth that announced, "Proper job."

With long, scaffolding planks to lessen the angle and ropes to roll the tarpaulin-wrapped seal up onto the tailgate, we struggled, sweating as the sun burst through again. Seal successfully lifted brought forth a tenner, which I happily trousered and reminded Derek we'd agreed more. He said it would be £2 for unloading, too and a further £3 for digging the new hole, total £15. Canny lad. We set off with a thumbs up out the van window to his mother, who was holding her nose with a lace napkin. The council would pay Derek for taking the seal off the beach and also pay him for disposing of it.

"Where will he put it?" I had asked Mrs Clifton, expecting a guarded answer.

"Oh, he'll dig it into the roots of a grape vine; he's been asked."

"Whereabouts? Pendeen?"

"Oh, he won't say, better that way."

I would later discover the destination was usually an artist's garden near Pendeen. He would be paid by the vine owner for excavating the hole, digging in the seal and also taking away the unwanted earth. That's four payments: off the beach, disposing, digging in, earth-disposing.

"He knows someone who'd like the earth he's collecting, too," she added.

"My God, five payments." I shook my head in wonderment and admiration. Still, my £10 for an hour's asphyxiatingly smelly work, whilst simultaneously being paid on duty, was welcome. Plus, the £2 and £3 made £15. Derek had also offered to take me with him mackerel fishing the following morning. That'll be a few fish for me, add some baked potatoes, and I can have a beach party tomorrow evening. Better collect some driftwood, phone around a few friends and let's hope tomorrow morning's fish co-operate.

Towards the end of the season – the water warm, the days still longish, the surf building towards autumn, on a Friday afternoon, just before bed-changing Saturday in the world of B&B – a bare-chested Birmingham chap struggled up my sand dune. I knew he was a Brummie as he'd been sunburnt whilst wearing his string vest, so without it, he looked like he was still wearing it. From his bottom lip hung an ash-tipped cigarette. Out of breath, he hissed, "Av losst me fausse teeff."

"Pardon?"

"Av losst me fausse teee-eeeff."

"You've lost your false teeth?"

"Yefff"

"Whereabouts?"

"Fumwere back in i dune-sss, ah hink. A'v looked evryware."

"OK, I can ask everyone; I'll get the megaphone. Both sets, top and bottom?"

"Yefff, a awways takes em out to gi me gums a refft, like."

"OK, let's go." We walked the length of the beach twice, people smiling at my megaphone's strange request, but all the visitors were heading for dinner. No luck. "Sorry about that. I can take your B&B number and call you later after I've had a good search."

"Dunno B&B's nummer."

"OK, just give me your name and address. Later this month, we get strong winds that'll reveal the teeth. I'll post them on to you."

"Gie'ff a pen." He wrote slowly and handed me the paper.

"Almost guaranteed to find them, unless someone steals them, ha, ha," I laughed.

He gave me a sad, baleful look and I smiled encouragingly. His wife appeared. "Ee's lost 'em before, you know." She hauled him away, looking back, saying, "And it's sirloin steak for dinner tonight, his favourite!" His expression turned from baleful to doleful.

I wasn't too hopeful of finding his teeth as the season's end approached and things bury themselves deeply in sand, however, after a few days of wind, I had another concentrated search and, strangely enough, half-hidden behind rocks, away from his indicated area, nestled a perfect set of nicotine-stained dentures. Funnily, I still had his address tucked in my logbook, and after careful wrapping in wind-tossed 'Tory rags', I posted them at Sennen's tiny, part-time Post Office.

The girl weighed them. "A present for someone?" she queried, one eyebrow raised, hoping for some romantic gossip.

"No, a set of lost dentures, second-class, the postage, I mean, not the dentures." I paid and left; she smiled. Perhaps that was enough gossip for a small P.O.

Five days later, I received a letter from the Birmingham area, kept for me at the café, which was effectively my 'poste restante'.

"Letter from someone nice?" queried Mrs Clifton, one eyebrow raised, hoping for some romantic gossip.

"No, it'll be a thank you from a visitor." I tore open the envelope. "Weirdly, I found his lost dentures and posted them on... and even more weirdly... they're not his..." I read the note, laughing sympathetically. His wife had included two pound notes for postage. Even weirder, I think I found them two seasons later, worn down by the constantly moving sand. No point in sending again; they'd been lost too long in the 'sands of time' and not suitable to chew sirloin steak.

Our mackerel fishing was postponed, too rough, but the following Wednesday was forecast ideal: tide right, gentle wind, we would launch at 6am, first light. I would be back in time to start work. Derek had long lines with many hooks prepared, plus some bait for cod. Mackerel are happy to bite

Kenny sailing, unstormy day, there's fish down there

on just the flash of a bare hook and they swim not too deep, pelagic, a new word for me. A wonderful, oily fish, quick to prepare, no significant bones and easy to cook provided it's fresh, best at one day old. Derek-the-profiteer preferred cod and hake, more value, commanding a higher price. I would be happy with free mackerel and just enough time to plan a BBQ in the sand dunes with jacket potatoes and nearly fresh bread, washed down with pints of St Austell's Ales.

We launched Derek's five metre boat, his small outboard puttering obediently behind, being overtaken by the local creel boats, coughing as their diesel engines churned.

"Your boat doesn't go very fast," I noted, wishing to return in time for work.

"No, but tidn't costin' me much, neither, boy." He smiled. "Specially as you're not contributin' nothin' to this venture. Your surfboard don't go very fast, neither, when you're paddlin' out."

"True, but my surfboard costs nothing at all and takes me to Heaven and back for free," I countered.

"I thought that was your girlfriends what took you to 'eaven and back." Occasionally, there was a hint of unadmitted jealousy in Derek's comments.

For all his fast-accumulating wealth and his status in the lifeboat crew, he was shy with girls and suspected that all 'stoodents' were hedonists with enough free time to match. I smiled to acknowledge his remark and gloried in the fact that it was mainly true. Life was good and full, but a sudden hook in my finger brought dark red blood spurting its reality. Derek laughed. "Don't worry, boy, it's not an artery. You'll be all right dreckly." With a pair of pliers, he cut both ends from the hook and pulled it through.

I breathed deeply through flaring nostrils, dropping my bleeding hand into the cold sea. "Oooh that's better. Cooler and less pain," I gasped.

"Brings sharks though, boy," laughed Derek. He took great amusement from any discomfort on my side, ever the vulnerable 'stoodent'.

The sun shone, peeking over the cliffs and, with the engine now cut, we lolled off Land's End, rolling lazily on glassy water, only one of us bleeding profusely into reputedly shark-filled waters.

"On they oars, boy," Derek commanded as he started to lay the long lines while I rowed, silently pondering the long winter in the city which would follow this coming autumn. We had been busy baiting some lines and chatting when suddenly, absolutely nothing happened, just silence, a few distant gannets diving crazily from on high.

I looked around, impressed by the towering overhangs of Mayon Cliff, three hundred feet of solid granite rock. As we drifted closer, I could see the sad remains of the rusty hull of the *Jeanne Gougy*, a Brest trawler that had made an elementary mistake in 1962. The crew had been fishing non-stop for several days and, exhausted, had engaged their simple autopilot; it could steer a heading but not navigate. The skipper was not alert approaching Land's End, exhaustion always brings mistakes, and the boat hit a well-charted and well-named danger: the Shark's Fin Rock. Picture the shape: one side sloping, the other vertical. Depth could be sensed by the boat's echo sounder, but its alarm would be short and too late when approaching from the vertical direction. From this direction, the warning would have sounded exactly as the boat hit. With the alarm beeping, immediately followed by a crunching noise, the sleep-deprived skipper staggered to the bridge, aware that his beloved boat was now taking on water. In the darkness, believing he was just off Whitesand Beach, he turned and set full power, planning to beach her and save the crew, perhaps even the boat herself. Many a boat has run up a beach and been saved. Fatally though, he was not off Whitesand; he was exactly under Land's End and hit the cliff at full power, helped by huge waves and a following wind, ripping her keel open.

The boat was pounded and quickly broke up. Arriving later, the Coastguard peered in the dark, down under the three hundred-foot cliffs. Nothing could be done until daylight and a breeches buoy had been erected. For three days, the coastguard tried to reach the boat, which was rolling violently in the waves, pinning it to the sharp rocks. When conditions abated slightly, a small dog was seen in the cockpit and a breeches buoy was launched down.

As a twelve-year-old child in 1962, I used to cycle the fifteen miles from St Ives, and back most days to watch, rapt with the drama of men trying to reach the boat. The coastguard finally brought up only dead bodies. The coffins of these Breton fishermen were carried through Newlyn, the road lined with local fishermen and their families, watching their own potential fate through tear-rimmed eyes. At our school, prayers were said in assembly, the hymn 'For Those in Peril on the Seas' was sung with many of us sobbing. These men were strangers, but they were also us, a fishing community, always aware of shipwrecks. I reminded Derek of this tragedy only nine years later whilst we fished. "Fssff," he sucked. "Nice propeller, phosphor bronze and a pretty ship's wheel."

I was outraged, but with people like Derek, the tradition of Cornish wreckers dies hard. He may only have been kidding, but he said no more, leaving me to my silent moral dilemma. We continued our fishing.

"Derek, what's the difference between privateers, pirates, wrecking and smuggling? They all seem a bit dodgy."

"Well, privateers is stealing from foreigners like the Spanish on behalf of the Crown. Helps the Navy. Whereas, pirates is privateers but on their own behalf, see? Crown don't get a bit. Navy'll chase pirates for a bit of practice. Rubs the rust off their guns."

"And wrecking?" I queried.

"An' wrecking is taking valuable bits of cargo off an abandoned boat. Crown might get a bit. Navy's not interested, dangerously close to shore for 'em. An' finally, smugglin's shippin' cargo into the country without tax or duty. Crown don't get a bit. Navy'll chase smugglers but not close to shore. The Cornish are all of the above, often at the same time if they's clever. Keeps their 'eads down and their eyes out, see?"

"And what are you then, Derek?" I tilted my head, accusingly.

"Oh, I'm just an innocent fisherboy, so I just keeps my 'ead down and my eyes out, see?" smiled Derek with a satisfied grin.

I'd just been outwitted in another conversation. I'd never get a straight answer. Derek was correct – it's better to salvage what's salvageable.

French Trawler Jeanne Gougy, 1962,
credit Memorial National des Marins

Suddenly, 'doing nothing' stopped its lazy happening; the lines were energetically alive with mackerel and we hauled them in. Derek could flick them off the hook with his practised ease while I just yanked them off. Now, even Derek's cod lines were busy and he left me to the low-value mackerel. The scuppers were alive with fish, and I was starting to feel queasy. It's, urghh, time for home. Scuppers full, we pootled homewards as I looked rearwards, Longships with its far-reaching light and foghorn and the Seven Sisters Rocks, both traps for the unwitting.

Gutting and cleaning speedily, I still had time to vomit over the side, ironically attracting more fish, and then, feeling slightly better, we approached the cove's tiny harbour. A settled high-pressure area means light winds so near the top of my sand dune would be fine for the fire, and widdling would be in the dunes. Buy some Bacofoil and tatties, mackerel in butter and foil, potatoes wrapped in foil and buried in the sand with the fire built over it.

A few phone calls to mates: "Old Success this evening, a few pints, a game of skittles, then to my hut 'bout ten o'clock. Bring drink, driftwood, your girlfriend and any sisters, guitars always welcome." A party on the sand dunes tried to follow the recommended advice of naval experts:

> *Now let ev'ry man drink off his full bumper*
> *And let ev'ry man drink off his full glass;*
> *We'll drink and be jolly and drown melancholy*
> *And here's to the health of each true-hearted lass.*

'SPANISH LADIES' (TRAD. 18ᵀᴴ CENT.
NAVAL SHANTY FROM PENINSULAR WAR).

Only one girl for me, though; I was looking forward to Helen coming tonight: grace, beauty and tenderness; maybe I should become a farmer after all...

Hungover 'guests' needing tea and coffee

The sweetest hours that e'er I spent
Were spent among the lasses o.
ROBERT BURNS, 'GREEN GROW THE RASHES'.

The following morning, I wandered over to the car park while my 'house guests' recovered from a night in the sand dunes.

Seeing John, I called out three more guesses of his surname, "Pool, Wirral, Mersey?"

John laughed, shook his head and sauntered over, his limp and beard giving a Cornish character to his Liverpudlian humour, although he'd only been two seasons here. John was always keen to have an oblique conversation which would lead to insights or confusion. "Here, what's this surfin' really like, then?"

"Well, how to explain? Let's see, do you know anything about drag racing? It hardly exists in the UK, but it's popular in the US."

"Is it anything to do with men dressed as women?" he ventured cautiously.

I examined his face for signs of a suppressed laugh – he was expressionless. "No, nothing to do with men or women, it's a competition of the fastest acceleration over a short distance; they have specially built dragsters to race."

"And so?"

"And so, there's the world champion, Gary Gabbelich, in the US, who was asked a similar question by a TV journalist, 'Gary, for our viewers, what's drag racing really like?'"

"So, what did he answer?"

"Gabbelich's answer was, 'It's better than drugs; it's better than sex, man; it's better than anything.'"

"Did this Gary guy get in trouble for uttering such immoralities in the Land of Capitalism and the Freely Sanctimonious?"

"No, apparently they edited it out. Drag racing is dangerous enough without inviting the Confederates' version of a fatwa."

"So, finally, what's surfin' really like, then?" said John with irritation.

I tilted my head. "Well, my friend, it's even better than drag racing."

John hooted his appreciation. "God, I wish I were young again!" He stomped off, repeating my answer, "...it's even better than drag racing." John pivoted on his good leg and shouted back, "Ey, wack, your friend Steve was 'ere earlier, gone down to Land's End now, but he'll pop down again about midday."

"Steve who?"

"Steve-I'm-a-mate-from-uni. Irish girlfriend, very striking, nice clobber," he replied with a wink.

That narrowed my two Steves down to one: uni-Steve with his girlfriend Finna, down from London. Amazingly, today's other visitor would be Concorde. The local newspapers and radio had flagged in advance the trial flight of the new Anglo-French Concorde, down the Cornish coast for the first time, weather permitting. I was looking forward to this visit. In November last year, the two test Concordes had reached Mach 2 (1,350mph) for the first time, within a few days of each other; soon they were testing daily. With improved Olympus engines, they could maintain Mach 2 cruise speeds over previously unheard of distances, a sphere of test flying previously unexplored. A Concorde's supersonic flight time is much longer than a brief military aircraft burst, so many new design problems had to be anticipated, including high temperature, causing the aircraft and all its internal hydraulics and systems to s-t-r-e-t-c-h about six to twelve inches. The aeroplane would heat to 120°C, even though the outside air temperature at sixty thousand feet was -70°C. Today, the route chosen would be running in a north-south direction, eight hundred miles over parts of the western coasts of Scotland

and Wales, and over (yes!) Cornwall. Should I become a pilot? This question continually amazed me as I had never flown and knew almost nothing about flying. Why was I interested?

"D'you reckon we'll be 'urt by these 'ere sonic dooms?" queried John, interrupting my ambitious thoughts.

"John, I know that you know they're not 'dooms'; they're sonic booms, *booms*."

"The farmers say it'll make heifers, calves and bulls give birth," joked John.

I smiled and added, "Medically unlikely, but for sure, these Cornish farmers'll try and claim something against the government."

"These Cornish farmers are the poorest rich land-owning class in the world," moaned John, clicking his ticket machine and waving his crooked fingers to the next car.

So, Steve and his girlfriend Finna were visiting. Great, I liked them both. I popped into the café to borrow some biscuits and fresh milk. "Got some visitors coming today, Mrs Clifton – could I have some nice biscuits and fresh milk?"

Derek appeared by magic, holding a pint of milk and a packet of custard creams. "Proper job, boy, free, no charge, complementary and on the 'ouse, like."

My astonished face gaped at him. "Free from a fisherman?" I alliterated accidentally.

"Needin' some bricks moved and cement mixed, a five-hour job, startin' at first light in the mornin', twenty quid cash. You'll be back in time for work if you're quick."

"Call it twenty-five and I'll wear my best baggies," I haggled.

"Done! I'll be 'ere for you at four-thirty."

Milk and biscuits in hand, I crossed the beach. Steve was a great pal, a fellow mathematician who part-financed his uni course with the proceeds from his fearsome poker playing.

Setting a smaller bathing area than normal so I could police it more easily, I started tidying up my hut, brushing sand, wiping cups, towels drying outside on the sand. Binocs in hand, I checked the car park and, sure enough, Steve's Mini was pulling in; ten minutes for them to trudge across the beach. Steve represented the world I should be in: study, achievement and well-presented charm; ditto Finna. They would marry, that's certain, whereas I'll explore the planet before age overtakes me. Deep in our conversation, I occasionally remembered to watch the swimmers, conditions benign thankfully, sun shining, surf small with a satisfying sucking sound. Somehow, three hours passed; coffee, biscuits and milk almost finished, we all returned to the car park, giving me an opportunity to introduce capitalist Steve and communist John. I always seemed to straddle two cultures without entering either.

"Was great, wasn't it?" said John.

"What was great?" I asked.

"Concorde and the sonic doom."

"Oh, no! We didn't hear or see anything. When?"

"About an hour ago, no clouds, the whole beach saw it and heard the doom. Everyone was staring upwards. Didn't you see them?"

Saying a regretful goodbye to Steve and Finna as they disappeared up the hill in their stylish Mini, I turned to John. "I missed Concorde; maybe I'm not cut out to be a pilot – I'm too easily distracted."

"You'll pay closer attention when you're being paid, son, I guarantee you that," he laughed.

I turned away and then remembered. "My three guesses for today are Shankly, Kop, Anfield."

John shook his head and again predicted I'd guess eventually. As I trudged back across the beach, it was knocking-off time, the surf was rising, a pint and pasty afterwards and an early night before relieving Derek of £25 at dawn. Life has its compensations; don't ask for too much.

A few days later, I saw Helen trudging up my sand dune holding a small lad by the hand, not crying but with dried tears on his cheeks. She was comforting the wee boy and he smiled. Helen would be a natural mother when the time came. Her qualities were great practicality, empathy and beauty beyond compare. I would not deserve that until maturity conquered me later in life and by then it would be too late for us. How wonderful they looked together, aspiring mother and a child with a warm hand. She presented Jimmy with a gentle, theatrical flourish. "Here we have Jimmy and he'd like a dog, oh, and I told him we'd find his mother." Jimmy nodded enthusiastically, gazing up at Helen, wondering whether he should start crying again at the mention of his mother.

Kneeling down, I reassured him. "Yes, we find parents and children every day, even dogs if they're lost. Maybe we'll find a lost dog for you."

Helen found Jimmy a damp custard cream in my vanishing collection and he smiled shyly at my usual hangers-on of exhausted surfers and some girls awaiting the return of their own exhausted surfers. There was never any problem with lost kids, I just handed them over to someone's girlfriend and then I wandered the beach, bellowing through my megaphone until a distraught parent wept in my direction.

First, I lifted Jimmy to shoulder height. "Can you see where you were sitting?"

He gazed out, shook his head, put his head in my neck, started to cry and pointed behind him, a gesture that covered the whole beach. "OK, Jimmy, you have another biscuit and I'll go and find your mummy." Jimmy nodded, head nestled.

Helen told me that John the car park attendant had been given Jimmy. He'd kept Jimmy for ten minutes, issuing parking tickets furiously until he saw Helen heading for my hut. It was now 12.30pm, getting very hot, car park full, and no distraught parents yet. Very strange, normally the mother is weeping and staring around her in forlorn loss, other parents joining in the search. Helen now took Jimmy and sat him in the shade, playing a game.

I bestrode the beach with authority, calling for the parents. In the strong wind, every family had erected a windbreak so walking the beach takes some time, skirting these 'tents' of visitors. No result. I reached the café, alerted the staff, then to the car park, talked to John, and set off along the upper sand dunes. No result. I looked at my watch – 1.30pm. Jimmy must have been lost now for at least one hour. I called the Old Success nearby to explain and they promised to alert their staff. Back at the sand dune, I scanned the beach. Were there any abandoned towels or windbreaks; could the parents have silently drowned? Everything seemed normal and the time was now 2pm. I became busy with first aid and a reckless kid disappearing seawards on a lilo. Coming up the beach, I once more took the megaphone, another patrol. Jimmy was happily playing with my 'group' and learning everyone's name. Surfers come and go every twenty minutes, so Jimmy had now learnt many of their nicknames – there was 'Stoked', 'Hang Ten', 'Outside', 'Piglet' and others. Jimmy did well. I decided to give it another go megaphoning, no result, now 3pm. I called the police and explained the situation. They had no further information and their cars were too summer-busy to come out as far as Sennen. I explained that after finishing work, I'd have to take Jimmy on my motorbike to the police station at Penzance, no other option. Could they put out a call on local radio? Usually, it's lost kids, not lost parents. The police said 'yes' to the radio call-out but generally it's not successful until the beaches are emptying and car radios are on.

Jimmy would intermittently cry or laugh; he was tired and slept on my stretcher until 5pm. I worried for those two hours until I saw a couple with another two children coming towards my hut; they stopped below and shouted up, "You got our Jimmy, then?"

"Who are you?" I asked cautiously, stopping one of the surfers from fetching Jimmy.

"We're his parents, of course, Dopey, you were calling for us."

"Well, Dopey here would like your identification, and a very accurate description of Jimmy, before I let you see him."

"You can't stop us, mate," said Dad, now shouting threateningly from below the sand dune.

My group of surfers now rose from behind the dune's marram grass and looked down; they were surf-weary but very intimidating. At sight of them, the father suddenly became polite, described Jimmy and offered his driving licence. I noted all the details, and then the acid test was Jimmy's reaction as Helen carried him outside. He knew they were his parents but had already decided Helen was better. He reluctantly approached his 'loving' parents.

I looked at the father and said, "I'm not sure I should release Jimmy. Where the hell have you been for the last five hours?"

"We've been around; we just didn't notice Jimmy wasn't with us at the fish 'n' chips." By now, Jimmy was hugging his mother's leg.

"You won't be visiting this beach again," I said to Dad.

"You can't stop us, mate."

"I have your car number now and the car park attendant will be informed you don't park here ever again. You'd better be careful he doesn't thump you; he is boiling furious, and I'd watch out for the café owner and his son, too and all the staff of the Old Success, who are keeping an eye out for you as we speak."

The father and I stared each other down as Jimmy's mother dragged him off. "Time for dinner," she said, with Jimmy looking back longingly at his happy, surfing home.

Looking out to Scilly, the graveyard of countless ships, one particular marine tragedy flitted across my memory, a period of sorrow that had caused West Penwith to weep for the damaged beauty of Cornwall. Only four years before, as a fifteen-year-old, I'd cycled to a vantage point above Sennen to goggle at the Royal Navy jets strafing and bombing just over Land's End. Military jet aircraft were largely unseen in Cornwall, except for some maritime patrols by old, slow, propeller-driven Shackletons from Newquay. The Royal

Navy were deploying their Buccaneers and the Air Force their Hawker Hunters, suddenly called to drop the napalm that the British Government had recently denied possessing, stating clearly in the House of Commons: "In respect of concerns regarding the USA's use of certain weapons in Vietnam, I can state that we do not currently possess napalm." However, it turned out that the government did as, astride my bicycle, I had watched the Hunters coming in low, releasing bombs, incendiary bombs and, yes, napalm. As a young lad, this was fascinating stuff, excitedly watching a 'war' even as the whole of Cornwall was agonising over the 120,000 tonnes of oil pouring from the stricken tanker, SS Torrey Canyon, busy breaking her back on Pollard's Rock, a reef in the narrow channel between Land's End and the Isles of Scilly. What had happened to our rural marine idyll?

On Saturday, 18th March 1967, around 6.30am, the first officer of the three hundred-metre supertanker SS Torrey Canyon realised that his vessel was in the wrong place. He changed course, but when the sleep-deprived captain was awoken, he countermanded the order for schedule reasons; he was hurrying en route from Kuwait to Milford Haven. This was disastrous for the tourism of Cornwall, Brittany and the Channel Islands and massively fatal for local marine life. Most serious accidents have multiple causes, called the error chain. A series of mistakes or pieces of bad luck line up to allow disasters to occur. This ship was constrained by an unforgiving schedule, barely adequate charts, unhelpful winds and currents, the crew's confusion over the autopilot use and the appearance of fishing boats in her intended course. At the subsequent enquiry, these fishing boats were described as 'unexpected'. How can fishing boats be unexpected in the busiest and densest fishing grounds in Europe?

Later in life, as I was becoming a pilot, I often reflected on these avoidable problems: lives are more important than schedules, prior preparation ensures correct charts, winds and air currents are countered by skill, technical knowledge allows proper use of the autopilot and obstacles are to be expected in busy areas. The parallels of this 'easily avoidable' disaster were to guide my professional life in the skies.

On day one, the slick was eight miles long; by day two, it was twenty miles, the ripped hull vomiting tons of oil every minute. The oil quickly reached Brittany, which was now bearing the brunt of the slick, where it was known as the marée noire, or 'black tide'.

One strafing Navy pilot later commented: "The column of smoke from the burning oil went up to about twenty thousand feet. To continue bombing visually, we had to dive into smoke and flame." The *Torrey Canyon* broke in two and finally sank twelve days after it had run aground.

Concerned residents voluntarily squirted detergent from watering cans; fishermen were paid to pump chemicals into the sea from their boats, hoping to save some of their fishing livelihoods. The Army even punctured holes into barrels and rolled them uselessly off cliffs, adding to the damage. All of these made a bad situation much worse. The British plan was for the chemicals to break down the oil and allow it to disperse, finally being removed by natural bacteria. But instead, it killed any kind of marine life it came into contact with, from seaweed to limpets to fish. It took fifteen years for the treated areas to recover, about five times longer than those areas where the oil was dispersed naturally by wind and waves. The French had a gentler approach to nature, allowing the oil to come ashore onto their rocky beaches and then scooping it up, the remainder gradually weathering. As a result, their marine life was not as badly affected. Oil is, after all, just another hydrocarbon.

The horrific effects went on for years, damaging organisms from the bottom of the food chain, the plankton and small invertebrates that live in sediments, through mussels and clams up to fish, birds and mammals. The food chain became a chain of death. More than fifteen thousand sea birds were killed. Clogged up with thick, viscous oil, they were washed up dead or alive, often disabled and unable to breed, onto our previously pristine shores. Future populations of some species took decades to recover.

David Bellamy later stated: "At the time the *Torrey Canyon* went down, we were still considering the sea as the main place to put all our waste." This disaster led to changes in the way people viewed the environment, but supertankers and their incompetent crews continued to drive their ships onto rocks worldwide. As surfers, my pals and I remember the surf being like brown, gooey gravy, with the beaches themselves being coated by tar, misshapen lumps of it just 'every-bloody-where'. Cornwall has strong winds, and most smells are dispersed immediately, but this smell was oozing out every second, the overwhelming, carcinogenic nature of it making beachgoers lightheaded, dizzy and furious.

The remains of the *Torrey Canyon's* hull, having disgorged its poisonous contents to the four winds and tides, with a few slower, residual leaks, has finally, half a century later, become a hidden haven for marine life and divers.

In September, some surfing days are halcyon, with a long wave track

*Torrey Canyon, oil-spill 1967, credit
Alchetron, the free social encyclopedia*

over a gently sloping beach. The wave marches shorewards, steadily losing its power and would ordinarily topple over but is held up by an offshore wind, keeping it up, feathering the wispy tops, gradually weakening the wave's power. This leaves a translucent, tall, almost-vertical face the surfer can 'scoot' across, up and down, his surfboard causing its fragile face to tumble behind him, the wave finally breaking with spent force like an exhausted runner wobbling before collapsing at the finishing line.

Autumn '71 was now creeping up stealthily behind a happy summer. Helen was working at the Old Success as a chambermaid, and at summer's end, to add ecstasy to pleasure, Helen had hired a cottage flat overlooking the beach for late August and September. She installed her mynah bird, topically named Woodstock, a super bird, a Greater Hill Indian mynah. Mynahs are such perfect mimics that they can mimic anything, especially swear words, which they repeat endlessly in the accent, embarrassingly, of the original sinner. We had a squeaky front gate and Woodstock confused us by periodically squeaking, so we fruitlessly answered the door to a squeakily heralded, non-existent visitor until we twigged; it was the bird. Eventually, we didn't respond to the squeaks so arriving visitors assumed we were out and went away. Woodstock's 'pièce de résistance' was imitating the car next door, which often wouldn't start on cold mornings. With perfect replication, he would run the sequence of car door closing, engine turning over, a few engine coughs, a slowing starter, a few more coughs, the battery almost flat and the car door slamming again. Sometimes, for his secondary 'pièce de résistance', he would allow it to start and make vrooming sounds with much revving.

Rebuilding my Triumph T350 during the summer had not been easy in my sandy hut, with new piston rings, bearings, valves, chains, all being kept clean and lubricated. Sand is a death sentence for moving parts. Putting it all together after my efforts, I cautiously turned the engine a few times with the kick-start to bring through the first petrol, switched on the ignition, a firm kick and "Vrrooomm." Glorious success. I couldn't believe it; I sat overwhelmed on my bike, the engine idling quietly and evenly with the thought of all the engine parts, timing, cables, carburettors and my work synchronising beautifully. "Vrrooomm, vrrooomm," again. My summer work was ending; money had accumulated; Helen and I still had two weeks before uni recommenced, time for a driving holiday through Bodmin Moor and across Exmoor, to the Welsh mountains. Wales here we come, but we hadn't realised that in 1971, only married couples could share a room in a B&B in Wales! This concept was not lost on Helen.

After a rainy Wales, we were back in Sennen again, the big surf coming in early October, with the water still warm, often too hot, as I luxuriated in my home-made wetsuit, surfing alone with not another surfer to be seen.

Alone, alone, all, all alone,
Alone on a wide, wide sea!
SAMUEL TAYLOR COLERIDGE,
THE RIME OF THE ANCIENT MARINER.

Surfing alone in splendid late sunshine and autumn swells makes a full stop to a vanishing summer and now autumn is heralding winter.

With a heavy heart, Helen and I zoomed off to Southampton again – uni for me, waitressing for Helen – and Dave telling me yet again that I was treating Helen selfishly and that we'd split up. He was soon to be proved correct.

Our friendship had started to peter out as Helen left Southampton to return to Cornwall early. She couldn't see herself living 'across the Tamar' any longer. We shared no dramatic goodbyes, just a slow understanding, or misunderstanding. I mused on our relationship; perhaps it was like a tin mine, to draw a very Cornish parallel. Started with optimism, becoming successful and comfortably productive, eventually petering out in the face of diminishing returns, finally being shuttered against greater 'world' forces, never to be reopened but always looked upon with fondness, memories woven into our personal landscape, like mining's engine houses and Stone Age quoits, fondly regarded reminders of how history imprinted the land in times gone by.

Dave's criticism of my treatment of Helen was based on resentment, as he had always admired her. I treated her as a girlfriend and Dave expected me to treat her as a queen. She would have deserved that, but our lives were motoring on – Helen would want children soon, but not me, not yet. Helen would be someone else's wonderful wife.

I have loved thee for thy beauty,
But not for that alone.
BONNIE MARY O'ARGYLE (TRAD. FOLK SONG).

10

Summer 1972

Summer Days and Summer Nights...

Westering home, and a song in the air,
Light in the eye and it's goodbye to care.
Laughter o' love, and a welcoming there,
Isle of my heart, my own one.

TRANSLITERATION OF GAELIC FOLK SONG
'EILEAN MO CHRÌDH'.

The 1972 season started mid-June, so it was full throttle down the A30 to Sennen for a fourth summer of glory. If this was life then give me more! This summer start at Sennen was before my final uni exams were finishing, so a good friend Alastair agreed to fill in for me for a few days as I roared back to Southampton to finish off my last few exams, uninterested in the results. I'd already decided that maths was a dead end for me but the BSc (Hons) could be useful; it might impress employers even if I personally didn't. Although I couldn't know then that this would ultimately prove true, much to my advantage in the West Indies the following year.

The early summer rocketed faster than previous summers, and a hot, crowded August, day was coming to a sweaty close as the emets streamed up the hill. "Good, I can go surfing now, small surf but perfectly formed." A ragtag bunch of blokes were shepherding their mate up the sand dune towards me, the casualty holding his forehead. He looked pale but otherwise normal, however his supporting friends were looking colourless and aghast as they proffered him to me. I spotted a little bit of blood on his forehead, now oozing between his fingers and reached in for my first aid kit. He was trying to shake off his friends, but they still insisted on clinging to him, shoving him forwards to me.

"What's the problem?" I asked.

"Nothin'," he replied.

"It's 'is 'ead," his friends mumbled with hushed voices of dread.

More shoving forwards, more silent, shocked looks from his friends. I sat him down onto my red box of life-saving line, took some cotton wool and gently started prising his fingers off his forehead, the blood now becoming congealed.

"'s nothin'," he repeated to much stunned shaking of his pals' heads. "Wiz just leavin' the beach, goin' back to us B&B. Just tripped an 'it me 'ead on a rock." He sounded like he was looking forward to some fish 'n' chips. I was puzzled at his relaxed, painless demeanour and his pals' wordless staring, their goggling eyes pleading for me to perform an, as yet undefined, miracle.

Prising his fingers away gently, one by one, the sticky blood making it difficult, no new blood appearing, maybe it was healing already. Some of his pals looked the other way, others stared in horror of what was yet to be seen. Now I could see what they feared. In a bloodless hole in his forehead, I could see his brains pulsing gently, the skull bone having been pierced in a triangular hole. It was grey and dark inside; the contents moved, pulsing shards of broken bone. A friend was sick on the sand, I noted, to be covered later.

"You'll need to go to hospital," I said in even tones.

"Na, na, it's jist a cut."

"It's a bit worse than that. I'll patch it up to avoid infection then call an ambulance. If none is available, you'll need a lift to the hospital," I continued evenly, feeling a bit ill myself.

He tried to get up and his pals pushed him down. He started to struggle against them, and I realised he would increase his heart rate – not good in this situation.

"It's worse than you think," I continued.

He struggled to his feet, still game, so I reached in for my shaving mirror and held it up. He stared with saucer eyes then fainted and was instantly caught by his ever-vigilant attendants. Good, his heart rate was down. Some first aid and a hospital call were needed.

"Do you guys have a car?"

"Wy-eye, bonnie lad," came the Geordie answer with an urgent jangle of car keys.

The hospital receptionist explained that all ambulances were busy in heavy traffic and with holidaymakers falling off cliffs, having strokes, breaking legs and the usual mayhem of holiday resorts. With the thirty minutes transit time, it was best to drive him in.

"We'll stretcher him to the car park; someone run ahead, ready the car and reverse it to the café. Drive sensibly and head for Penzance town centre; you'll see the hospital signs; take him to the A&E entrance, remember A&E."

Walking back across the sand with my folded canvas stretcher, I saw the small rock they had gestured to, a small trickle of blood, already dark red, becoming black in the lowering sun. It was triangular and sharp. Kneeling down, I tried to pick it up; it seemed too small, but moving it was impossible as this Toblerone point was the 'tip of the iceberg', attached to the solid base rock of local terra firma, this piece being more 'firma' than necessary. There was no movement, no give, no wobble, just solid, deadly, triangular, sharp rock. I hoped he was getting good and speedy treatment.

Time to forget and wash away the day's trials in the swirl of the surf; now, "Where's that board wax?" Humming to myself, "I'm suited up and ready, just awaiting the left-hand break on the western shore." I looked up to check the surf and spied a kiddie's dinghy.

Plastic dinghies are fragile, cheap and seriously dangerous to health! When there was an offshore wind, I'd often advise the visitors by megaphone against using inflatables; an offshore wind is deadly for dinghies.

The usual event would happen when Daddy buys a dinghy for his beloved children. He proudly unpacks and inflates his new purchase and inserts the pathetic paddles for his uninitiated youngsters. Tempted by the warm, balmy, zephyr wind softly ruffling a smooth sea, he's unaware that this same light wind is only light because of the shelter of the hillside behind; it becomes stronger the further from land one ventures (and stronger as the day progresses). I'm already moving down the beach as they launch. An adult man has a good reach when his feet are firm in shallow water, holding a dinghy line, but as Daddy ventures further out, he starts to partially float, his apparent weight reducing. He cannot reach so far; his purchase on the sand reduces; he stumbles into a small hollow. Now Daddy is floating, but he loses the wet line as he uses his hands to 'paddle' upright. I'm starting to run. The line sinks, so now he's two metres from the three happy children giggling in their shiny, new dinghy as it heads seawards, slowly at first. Now I'm sprinting; I pick up my surfboard as I pass the waterline, not too fast now as stable breath will be important pretty soon. I throw my board into the water and jump aboard.

It's now a rescue in progress as I pass Daddy, floundering but still within his depth, just. The dinghy is floating faster now, his beloved children still waving to Daddy. We have a flat out race: dinghy versus surfboard. I'm stroking through the break, faster now; the children are beginning to look worried; the older one with armbands is slipping into the water shouting, "Daddy." I pass her as the now-lightened dinghy speeds up, starting to spin a little, the two smaller children clinging on and crying. It's starting to sail before the increasing wind, looking to flip. I'm just managing to gain on it; I pass the dinghy to the outside and block it. We're stopped. The children try and climb onto me, their saviour, but we're not all safe yet. The dinghy has too much windage to retrieve it, so I release and it turns, spins, flips and starts to skip with longer and longer hops. Bye-bye dinghy, Ireland here you come.

Now we are three! I stroke back to the older one. Now we are four on a submerging surfboard, but hard stroking brings its nose up, just enough. The wind is still blowing, and the shore is far with the added danger of losing the kids in the surf break, so I head across the wind towards the shelter of the rocks, knowing that I have a backstop at the distant pier if the wind strengthens further. As my breathing settles, I can hear the shrieking from the shore as they realise I'm heading for the rocks; I must reach there before the family clambers down and breaks legs. With slipping and sliding, I push the children 'round the ragged rocks' and they are enveloped in parental hugs. As I retrieve my board, Daddy has recovered and is asking, "What about our dinghy? It cost £3."

"You can fetch it anytime you pay a fisherman's time. Make sure he has a fast boat, lots of fuel and a powerful pair of binocs."

"Will we catch it?"

"No."

"Should I buy another?"

"No. My advice is stay in the shallows; lie in the shallows; play in the shallows." I sped off to discourage further indulgent, loving Daddies in balmy winds.

Triumph Roadster, rebuilt, then sold in 1972, it went to the USA, so did I in 1973

Planning ahead, I accepted a cousin's offer for my Triumph Roadster, my beloved rebuild. The only consolation was that these cars were indestructible and didn't rust, so perhaps I could buy it back in a few years. I didn't know then that he would sell it to a buyer in the USA and, by coincidence, I would also be in the USA. Any possessions not currently vital I would sell or give away, keeping just my bike and the Traveller until autumn.

The end of another season approacheth, holidaymakers less numerous, visiting surfers living in excited anticipation of the bigger autumn swells, all hoping the swells built before 'we had to head north again'. The water was warmer after the summer's steady heating, it would stay warmish until the end of October; people were saying goodbye to seasonal workers, a few last beers with a few straggling summer mates, the Old Success housemaids dwindling as the guest numbers reduced; I was counting the money I'd need for another impecunious year; if Sennen had any trees we'd have had swirls of leaves, but there were just the increasing swells bringing more seaweed for the farmers' potatoes. The equinoctial tides would be greatest soon; that would catch out a few strollers as they beachcombed at low tide; usually a tiring sprint in softening sand was enough to keep them safe and gave them a breathless conversation in the Old Success. "That tide'll catch ee out, see?" puffed an aged crone as he stumbled to his feet, readying a skittles shot. "An' runnin' won't 'elp at times, neither, my 'andsome, so beware."

Chris, owner of the local surf school, made the mistake of bringing down his Champ, a semi-military amphibious vehicle 'guaranteed' to be driveable in water. What a buzz! He chose a calm day, early evening, a warm sun descending, and his Champ roared down the beach belching fumes from its elevated exhaust stack. We gazed dubiously; usually these wizard vehicles are called military because they needed an army to keep them working properly. Chris buzzed up and down, in and out of the water, his elegant girlfriend in the passenger seat playing sunlit film star in dark glasses to Chris's grizzled unshaven actor, as they sprayed onlookers. This was great fun for all; we still gazed dubiously. Into the sea they went, chugging along just outside the shoreline, a small group of watchers cheering as they went, in, out, up the beach, down the beach, giving small kids rides, what fun! Chris was Cornwall's best-known hedonist, owner of Skewjack, his holiday surf village and disco, a big wave surfer, beloved general, all-round good egg with a limitlessly wide grin. We cheered as he zoomed along below the tideline, the low sun illuminating the Champ's spray; then he swung round wildly in an arcing crescent of sand to head up the beach, but the swerve dug him into some soft sand under the shallow water and the engine stalled. Generally, Whitesand Bay had firm sand, but there were softer patches and he'd found one in the shallows. No worries, start again, some misfiring and once more the engine stopped. Turning over again, more misfiring, battery ebbing, tide rising. Maybe we could push him up the beach, but the sand was becoming softer by the second; our feet were sinking as we heaved.

"Ee'll need a tractor for that dreckly," opined Derek, joining us, hands in pockets, with his wry smile hiding his suppressed glee. Derek's tractor would be hireable, I'm sure.

"C'mon, Derek, lend us a hand." We were eight persons heaving and shoving and all sinking deeper. Equinoctial tides rise rapidly, the water now above the axles. Cheerfully, Chris declared he'd come tomorrow with some tools to dry the electrics, plus a fresh battery – nothing to worry about, chaps.

"We 'ere idn't worried, Chris," added Derek unhelpfully.

So, the Champ was abandoned until first light when the tide would again be low. I couldn't be much help, but I rose early to be witness to future tales of distress or success and to note the results in my logbook. Chris appeared with his mechanic, jump leads, batteries and tools in a Land Rover MkI. Dog walkers stopped; gulls sat on the Champ's frame; the sun rose and warmed us. The tide allowed about one and a half hours of working time on firm sand. The mechanic seemed optimistic; he knew his machines.

"W'd 'ave been better if ee'd done it nearer 'igh tide, boy," offered Derek, appearing after his Penzance bread run. "Tractor job, this."

"Well, you've got a tractor, Derek, bring it down just in case." I tried to improve the situation.

He sucked his teeth. "Ffffhhhzz, mine's rented out, 'arvest season, see. Could fit 'im in tomorrow mornin' same time, plus forty-five minutes for tide. 'Alf-day 'ire, £30."

Chris was also optimistic. "We'll get it going; they're built for this; we don't need Cornish wreckers at extortionate rates of hire," he said, eyeing Derek. "Anyway, we've got the Land Rover here."

"Still needs a tractor and a long cable to get somethin' that weight out, I reckon, boy."

The mechanic ignored everyone, working steadily, then announced, "Let's give her a try."

The Champ started, firing on only four cylinders, much backfiring; he revved her and she died. Another start, same result, another repeat, and another...

The mechanic delved in again, the sea starting to lap round his wellies. "Oh God, looks like we need a new rotor arm." He raised his head in mournful regret. "Everything's OK 'cept the rotor arm. Maybe I can repair it for another try this evening. Sorry guys." He started taking the battery out.

"You'll 'ave to book my tractor now or it's double at the last minute cos I'll 'ave to postpone it for my mate's farm, 'arvest time, see, boy."

The tide rose rapidly so we all moved off. I'll probably have to explain this fast-submerging Champ to dozens of visitors and warn the surfers of a submerged obstruction. It would be invisible until the waves sucked back as an unlucky surfer sped across, chopping his legs off at the ankles. Maybe I'll attach a fisherman's orange float.

The evening low tide came and embarrassingly went. Visitors and locals gathered; the mechanic tried again but no luck.

"£60 for tomorrow mornin', I'll include the cable for free," smiled Derek, beaming at the Champ. Good-natured Chris nodded at Derek and gave a resigned grin; Derek Clifton wins the jackpot again.

Skewjack bus, Chris's surf school bus, 1972. Credit Terri Strick

The following day, squinting through the heavy rain from my lookout, I could just make out a tall, majestic figure, totally erect with a static appearance; this strange being was surfing, riding the waves with almost no movement. This could only be our Piglet, an ironic nickname. A large, paunchy figure held erect by a 5mm wetsuit. Piglet talked constantly about how he would soon be off to Hawaii, sometimes humming his home-made songs.

Soon I'm going to be, on the wild shores of Waikiki...

Piglet could surf like he sang, artlessly but adequately, without appearing to be in tune with his song or his waves. Conversely, buzzing back and forth across the waves' feathering faces were fit guys and scrawny kids, today's sudden showers of rain calming the wind's chop and smoothing the surface of the waves, a glassy day, the cloud rendering a grey uniformity that was almost ethereal. Piglet – still erect with a royal dignity, unseen since the Hawaiian princes invented surfing to impress their royal princesses – surfed across the waves until he and his dignity were wiped out by the shore break. Dignity retrieved, he slowly paddled back out with his regal stroke.

Shorts and shorty wetsuit quickly on, I ran down the beach, board under my arm. The forecast was for heavy showers with possible lightning as the day progressed. *It's dangerous to be the highest object when lighting develops*, I thought, but I happily expected Piglet to be our highest object and thus our unwary lightning conductor.

I smiled as I ran; Piglet had often spoken of his ambition to visit Hawaii and others had quietly joshed him about it. He was unlikely to save, plan and succeed in his lofty ambition, but dreams have a timeless value; we would allow him, with only a little affectionate ribbing.

"Hey, Piglet, when are you off?"

"Just getting my passport/visa/travellers cheques," he would proudly state as the unfulfilled months and years came and went.

I paddled out to the small group jostling for the best take-off position, the surf building. The waves were superb; the now-heavy rain was keeping visitors off the beach and we, in our wetsuits, could not possibly become wetter. At 10.30am, my autumn time for starting work, I revelled in effectively being paid to go surfing, provided the beach stayed empty. Professional surfer, in a small way. Life can be paradise if we take the time to cherish our particular, but rare, good fortune.

The rain became intermittent; heavy showers and the shafts of sunlight illuminated the building cumulonimbus. Maybe lightning would come soon. The waves diminished, also forecast, and everyone trooped towards my hut; a great morning had been taken on a rainy day. My hut floor was half concrete and half wood, so my dripping pals changed on the concrete part and, when dry, moved to the wooden floor, where we all crushed onto my stretcher bed and wobbly chair. Ten minutes later and last up the sand

Mike my assistant-lifeguard, watching for Piglet's safety, 1972

dune, toiling with his anachronistic longboard, was Piglet. He changed alone, standing in the puddle left by the others, when a loud crack of lightning hit my telegraph pole, shot down the wet phone cable, jumped the puddle and hit Piglet. He had just peeled his wetsuit down one leg and was standing on the other leg. Piglet screamed and hopped furiously, unable to place his other leg. We howled unsympathetically with helpless laughter. Calming down and rubbing his leg, Piglet revelled in his new-found notoriety: the man who had survived a lightning strike.

Nothing could stop him now – Hawaii here comes Piglet, singing no less, paraphrasing a surf song.

Happy times we've all been spending
We pray that every wave is never ending.

I checked the time and date, adding another entry to my logbook. A recovered Piglet warned, "You're not making me public in that logbook of yours, are ee? I'm supposed to be at work, took the day off sick."

"Piglet, you were almost famous before but now, after that lightning strike, you're officially immortal." Nothing could stop him now. Fame at last. Hawaii, beware.

11

Autumn 1972

Will I Grow Up to Be a Man?

As for me, I am tormented with an everlasting itch for things remote.
I love to sail forbidden seas, and land on barbarous coasts.
ISHMAEL IN HERMAN MELVILLE'S *MOBY DICK.*

I was very healthy then, but I needed to be sure about eyesight. A pal's girlfriend was an optician's assistant, and she tested my eyes on the sly, for free. Oooh, astigmatism, I would need an expensive, professional assessment, so £35 lighter and a week later, I got the official result. Slight astigmatism was the verdict, in my right eye.

A prescription letter to British Airways produced their considered reply:

"You'll need spectacles at around the age of thirty; that's when eyes generally will change again."

"Again?" I worried.

"Yes," explained the optician the following week. "They change mostly at age eleven and then again at age thirty. After you reach fifty, your eyes will deteriorate slowly as you age."

A phone call to BA's recruiter, "Does that mean I cannot be a pilot as I'll need specs at age thirty?"

"No problem, many pilots have specs; they just need their sight to be correctable and carry two pairs of glasses when on duty."

"Yahooooo! So, pilot it is – here I come. When do I apply?"

"You don't; we're not hiring. Busy yourself and apply every year. Good luck," the recruiter replied sympathetically.

"In that case, I'll sell everything and go to the Americas. See you later, aviator," I joked.

I lent my Morris Traveller to Mick's wife as they emptied their caravan home and sold their furniture, preparing to emigrate. They were packing, selling their 'stuff' and steeling themselves for a new life. I knew Mick would prosper in Oz as he was handy, quick to learn, a stranger to academia but able to fix anything. With three weeks before departure, Mick then sold his T500, so I lent him my T350 bike, which meant I was now 'confined to barracks' as they had all my transport; bike and car. Friends are friends, sayeth I. Mick and his wife were still working at the meadery, and when he returned my bike, it was still two weeks till their departure, and I was standing chatting to Sandy when Mick appeared, astride my bike.

"Many thanks for the bike. Open invitation for you and any partner at the meadery," announced Mick. "Free food and drink till we leave. Just be a bit discreet in the restaurant and look like you're paying with a cheque."

Accepting his dodgy offer immediately, I turned to Sandy. "Dearest Sandy, would you care to accompany me this evening to partake in chicken in the bucket, washed down with a gallon of Cornwall's finest mead wine?"

"Don' mind if I does, kind sir," curtseyed Sandy, and thus we ate for free several evenings during the next two weeks, weaving back from Pendeen to Sennen with Sandy on pillion, thanking God that my bike remembered every devil's elbow corner on this dark and rainy road. It even knew when to draw in and drop Sandy at her door, a chaste shouted goodnight, and down the hill into the darkness.

As usual, she would be walking her dogs tomorrow morning and maybe we would chat. Sandy was a delightful girl and super company. I have often wondered why wonderful Sandy and I never became intimate friends, but we didn't and thus still remain friends today, even in the gloaming of our lives.

Luckily, I didn't know then that I would never see Mick again; that would have been too upsetting. He and I had been very close, with motorbikes, squash, and lifeguarding cementing our friendship. I explained to Mick's parents that I just couldn't bring myself to say goodbye in person.

I met Lucy near the end of season; she was summer chambermaiding in the Old Success so, for me, that meant a frequent warm bed and free room-service meals. Lucy was amazed that I knew my way around the odd wiring and idiosyncratic plumbing of her room, in the rabbit's warren of the hotel and its staff quarters, but that, strangely, I knew none of the housekeeping staff. That was because I'd been there only at night, after closing time. Coincidentally, she had Helen's old room; hard to explain that!

I had met Lucy by what I called a 'beach chance'. She was sitting on a rock, sketching the sea, erasing and retrying. I'd seen her waitressing in the Old Success restaurant, sometimes in the bar. As I walked up, I knew her sketch would be commendable but poor; Cornwall is full of excellent artists who cannot draw or paint waves. As she erased another attempt, I volunteered, "You need to understand how the wave forms, then breaks, then dissipates. Art is the same as everything in life, it requires the closest observation."

"Oh, does it?" she started with friendly sarcasm, not turning round. "An aspiring artist wouldn't know that!"

"Well, a small child observes something new with an intense concentration – that's why children learn so quickly and we don't," I offered, but she looked back, unimpressed. Unabashed, I continued, "See how it feathers and then breaks at one point and the break travels along? Sometimes, if the beach is flat, it breaks all at the same time. A wave dashes itself into a zillion bubbles that progressively dissipate. Now, watch the constant arrival of coming waves, in different stages of development. Take care not to stare too long; lines of waves become mesmeric."

She silently studied the waves then dropped her sketchpad, and we walked into the smaller surf and I lifted her weightlessly upwards, synchronising with the wave, and allowed her to sink into the foam. She shrieked and then relaxed, helping her greet the next waves. "Feel the motion of a thousand miles," I advised, almost poetically, warming to my topic.

I released her again, she dropped and then surfaced waist-deep further along, her nostrils blowing foam, her make-up weeping like a clown's. "You bugger! It's air bubbles, not water at all," she spluttered.

"You can only understand how to sketch foam by immersion. We call it 'soup', by the way."

She calmed. "I got the message; you're a good teacher."

"Maybe so, maybe not, but I'm not teaching art, just an understanding of waves."

Happily, she pushed herself along with the next wave, doggy-paddling, floating free and cheerily stumbling onto the shore. Chilled, she had to leave and prepare for serving dinner at the Old Success. "Many thanks for the free lesson," she laughed, dripping in her flapping shorts and clinging fishermen's smock. Picking up her sketchpad, she scurried towards the pub but turned quickly. "What will you teach me next time?" she shouted.

To my own surprise, I blushed for the first time in my life. "How about the feel and form of warm sand dunes?" I hazarded. I scolded myself; if I see her again, then I'll tell her I'm leaving Cornwall, I promised my better self, unconvincingly. I looked towards the sea. I'll miss this wonderland. With their incessant arrivals, waves are both temporary and eternally timeless.

Liverpudlian John was finishing his season, so today was my last guessing chance. "Liver, Scouser, Everton?" I called.

"No, wack, but you'll guess it eventually." We said our goodbyes with briny tears running down our hairy faces. "We'll always have Casablanca," he hooted inaccurately.

September and October, the water is at its warmest, halcyon days of great surf in autumn's heavy swells. I was still doing some building site work for Derek, so the bank account was swelling nicely with my summer's wages and some remains of my grant, as I awaited my annual tax refund for having worked only three months. Need cash to travel. By the way, what's a traveller's cheque? I'd decided to sell my surfboard, bike and my Morris Traveller prior to getting a student ticket to the USA, open for one year. Nothing was planned after that.

Saying goodbye to beloved Sennen Cove

Lucy and I said our long goodbyes, spending a few days walking in the warm autumn sun. "Well, at least you helped me draw waves and sand dunes," she said evenly with reproach. "What would you teach me if we should ever meet again?"

Looking back, I blushed for the second time in my life. "I don't know, maybe an understanding of clouds?" Neither of us could guess that, one year hence, I would send her a 'Letter from America' to say 'come over, let's meet in Canada'.

As a suitable adieu to my fast-becoming previous life, I unwisely decided to risk paddling round from Sennen to Nanjizal Beach, under the massive cliffs of Land's End itself.

"You'll be back dreckly if Jan Tregeagle sees ee, boy," laughed Derek as I told him my sketchy plan but not the date.

The distance is three miles, making six miles return, which I calculated would take about three hours, a bit more with a snack and short rest at Nanjizal. The winds, currents and tides are fearsome, so I'd selected a calm day, no significant swell, and aimed for slack tide under Land's End, all during a warm afternoon. I was sure no one had tried this foolish adventure before on a surfboard, a caper made more stupid by not telling anyone in advance, so with only a wetsuit for safety, no radio, I set off, propelled by dread and disquietude. "Am I a man or a mouse?" I squeaked to myself as I paddled. The naval maxim 'Fear God and Dread Nought' flitted across my mind, soon to be replaced by awe at the cliffs. I passed the Iron Age fort of Mayon Castle peeking just over the cliff edge; I spotted the remains of a recent wreck, the *Jeanne Gougy*; and, passing inside of Longships, I approached Land's End itself. Looking up, I could see a few end-of-season tourists dangerously peering over from above. Being right close under the cliffs, I couldn't see even the roof of the Land's End Hotel, but my memory reminded me of the mileages emblazoned on a post near the hotel. It was 3,147 miles from New York and 874 miles from John o'Groats, or was it 784 miles? The tide being high about now, I could pass between the jagged rock called The Armed Knight and the Enys Dodnan Arch. I'd later look up the meaning: *enys* meaning 'circle' or 'island', *dodnan* meaning 'with the soil on it', and it was true: all the other rocks here are devoid of soil. The Enys Dodnan arch's opening wouldn't be visible until my return paddle could give me the correct angle. A light tailwind had sprung up, somewhat welcome after one hour of paddling, with only thirty minutes to go. Ignoring Carn Boel, I could now see my turn-around point, Nanjizal, often associated with the forewarned demon, Jan Tregeagle.

I landed my board in Nanjizal's tiny sandy cove, unwrapped my still-hot pasty and accidentally disturbed a young couple, the hidden coves around here being ideal for intimate romance. Slightly embarrassed, they quickly invented a conversational question about Cornish pasties. I told them, "Popeye has spinach and the Cornish have pasties. Gives strength and endurance." They told me they planned to try a pasty and a drink at the hotel bar on the way back, until I warned them of the demon, Jan Tregeagle. Jan's name is well-known and feared in West Cornwall as his wild spirit rages on the coldest, darkest nights, his screams being heard on the winds along the rugged coasts, across craggy headlands and through dark, wooded valleys. Jan Tregeagle's spirit can never rest, since in life he was perhaps the most evil man the Duchy has ever known and was famed for forging a pact with the Devil. To assuage his sins, he was given the Sisyphean task of sweeping the sand from Porthcurno Cove, around the headland of Tol-Pedn-Penwith into Nanjizal Bay, and there he continues with his task, never-ending because the currents return the sand forthwith. On many a winter night, if 'ye tarries awhiles long' in the Land's End bar and then you set off along the cliff path to Sennen, you can hear the demon howling and roaring, tugging at your clothes. That's Jan Tregeagle. Having known several locals who swore, with fear in their eyes, that Jan had chased them, I myself never did tarry after dark.

Pasty now finished, I pushed my surfboard out, seeing the young couple hurrying up the crumbling cliff path. "Don' be late now or Jan'll catch ye," I called out encouragingly in my best Cornish accent. Clutching each other, they sped onwards and upwards. Congratulating myself on a scary tale well-told on behalf of the Cornish tourist board, I noted the headwinds now confronting

Paddling from Nanjizal, under Land's End, inside the Longships, beware Jan Tregeagle

me, choppy waters rising. Can Jan catch me on the water? I knew ghosts couldn't cross water, but Jan was not a ghost; he had actually existed, being an evil seventeenth century magistrate, and then later became a demon for his sins. Best to return before the wind increased and darkness fell. Approaching Enys Dodnan from the south-east, its arch hole was clear but no time to stop. I paddled on, the clouds gathering, now seeing the flashing Wolf Rock Light standing sentinel on its single rock, eight nautical miles to the south-west; late September on a cloudy evening can be gloomy. Rounding Land's End, passing inside of Longships again, the wind came abeam, giving me some relief and, with pasty-powered energy, I paddled towards the few lights of Sennen Cove, the Old Success Inn just coming into view. Darkness descending, I caught a helpful wave, then dragged my board from the deep; two beers, another pasty and a game of skittles awaited, still dripping my wetsuit onto the granite floor. I loved this cove. Jan Tregeagle will need to wait for another night but then, he has all of eternity until cometh the Day of Judgement.

As I walked by the tideline one evening so fair
To view the salt waters and take the salt air...
'FIDDLER'S GREEN' (TRAD. 1850S SAILOR'S SONG).

The summer had ended, the autumn surf was bigger, warmer, the beach almost deserted, and sunsets seemed to herald lyrical moments that are with me still, fifty plus years later. Romance may have come and gone, but my long-lasting love for storm-washed, granite-strewn Cornish cliffs remains still.

Till a' the seas gang dry, my dear,
And the rocks melt wi' the sun;
I will love thee still, my dear,
While the sands o' life shall run.
ROBERT BURNS, *A RED, RED ROSE.*

I'd slept well but my ears were aware of that wind which had tugged all night at my stout, wee hut, passing through the gaps and rustling at my flimsy blankets; autumn beckons. I'd hoped for this wind as my time was limited; recent nights had passed untroubled by the wind. Finally, my desired wind had arrived overnight, strong, dry, onshore, it pleasured me in my satisfied sleep, whispering to my monitoring unconscious: "Awaken early and receive your unearned autumn reward." Now, the rising sun, not yet over the cliffs, glistered the broken clouds and tinted the sky. I could see my long-awaited tiny pyramids of golden sand. At summer's end, the autumn winds increase, pushing the sand, grain by obedient grain, up the beach, sweeping towards the dunes and revealing beneath that which is heavier. By a quirk of aerodynamics, atop these pyramids lay coins of the realm, perfectly horizontal: bright sixpences, brown thrupenny bits, grubby pennies and dulled shillings. The winds had done their energetic night shift. I gathered these in my pockets. Speed mattered, for soon the dog walkers would arrive with the early morning and dogs would heedlessly brush these coins back into the sand. I moved quickly; in two hours I could gather the equivalent of one month's wages (tax free!). For the moment, these are truly Cornwall's golden sands.

Countless holidaymakers had dropped a few coins. Throughout the summer, gentlemen often sat in their serge trews, a few coins spilling from their pockets. Small children had dropped their change as they clutched their 'real Cornish' ice-cream cornet closely and stumbled back to Mummy. Mummy also dropped a few as she put the remaining change into her purse. On sand, people are often off-balance, I gloated. Young lovers rolled behind the dunes and their torn Levis dribbled pocket money. For this was the Swinging '60s, when money was all in coins of the realm and pockets had no Velcro or zips. Coins do not drop and lie helpfully in your gaze; they spear themselves into the welcoming sand. For an alert young lifeguard, this was the Bank of Sand. "All summer long, I've waited for you..." and now the coins were visible for the picking.

I sped along from the café to the far end of the beach, ahead of any perchance dog walkers. My canvas baggies' pockets were bulging and heavy; soon I'd have to empty, but I would fortuitously pass my hut, sitting midway along the beach. Thus, I could 'fleece' the beach in four cloverleaf, lucky loops, each loop completing at my hut, empty the coins again and start another loop. *Loop the loop*, I thought, not realising that I would accomplish this during later flying training. Free money, an end-of-season bonus, luck of the Irish, but today, luck of the Cornish.

Working as a lifeguard had been four bountiful summers, fitting perfectly into uni hols; I could earn nicely, spend only thriftily, live in my wee hut, entertain passing lovelies, go surfing early mornings and late evenings, earn extra by weekly litter-picking, bury the odd dead seal, find coins on sandy pyramids, topped off by the end-of-season tax refund for a poor student.

Seeing Derek's Land Rover, I went over to say farewell. He looked rueful and we slowly shook hands. "I bid you farewell and wish you good fortune, Derek," I smiled.

He laughed, "Yes, good fortune it is cos I just been put on the council's Approved Suppliers List. That means some good contracts by next winter. When you comin' back, boy?"

"Well, about thirteen months from now, after my American travels – I'll be broke by then."

"You'll be on-site with me at Marazion; we'll be startin' the sea wall early '74, big job. You, me, Big Jim and Maurice, three months work likely." He grinned at the thought of 'some 'ansome profit'.

"Derek, I'll wear my heavy-duty baggies and steel-capped flip-flops." I laughed, we shook again and he drove off.

I scanned the empty beach, now devoid of troublesome 'vacanciers'. The word 'zen' had only just entered the Cornish vernacular. Yes, zen was the feeling given by an empty beach, looming cliffs and upwelling waves. Maybe we should rename it Zennen? I had seen yesterday's forecast; there should be some big surf coming later today. Pray for an offshore wind and nirvana will unite with zen to produce Shangri-La. Was I inadvertently becoming a hippie? *No, I'm rooted in Mammon and Nature*, I thought as I trousered several half-crowns and sped to the café for a tasty breakfast of yesterday's pasty, given freely by Mrs Clifton to this impoverished student with a winning smile.

The heavy swells came as forecast and I paddled out alone, feeling slightly nervous as the big sets were lining up outside. Taking advantage of the rip current, I skirted round the peaks and sat ready to ride the next set. There was no one to aid me if a wipeout was dangerous. Here comes the next wave, its peak feathering enticingly. I catch it, drop in, turn, cut back for another turn, up to the lip, drop in again, bounce off the foam, turn again, kick out and paddle back out to the take-off point again. I'm not yet dead; I'm king of the universe. I considered my philosophy of life: 'I'm gonna live forever or die in the attempt'. Thank you again, Spike Milligan. He made dying sound heroic. Now, here comes another wave.

You'll be pleased to know I survived that thundering surf and so, with my passport, visa, and a Pan-Am ticket to Miami, I was busy saving money and preparing to go. Working for Derek, my end-of-season tax rebate and some farm work meant I had enough travellers' cheques for three months overseas, but after that, my options would be starve or work. Tearfully, I started to prepare for the western hemisphere: visa for the US; inoculations, like yellow fever for Latin America; a student's return ticket Heathrow-Miami-Heathrow, valid for one year; plus some of those vital travellers' cheques. I had Dave's contacts in St Lucia, my first destination, and his promise I could work there on his dad's building site, constructing hotels. What else could an optimistic student need? First, I would hitch-hike to visit Lucy near London, then sister Fiona in central London for a going-away party. The days were ticking to the end of a cold, wet December.

In fantasy land, you join the mile high club on your first flight in an aeroplane. Could that really happen? The world is definitely becoming my 'lobster'.

At the end of December, I set off from Cornwall, hitch-hiking to London; time to visit Lucy in Surrey and say goodbye as she went to uni. We both guessed that our summer tryst had come and gone.

> *Ae fond kiss, and then we sever;*
> *Ae fareweel, and then forever!*
> ROBERT BURNS, *AE FOND KISS.*

Thence to stay a couple of days with my sister Fiona. Before I left, Mother had given me two very small cases: one had enough space for a change of underwear, a pullover and my documents, the other was full of her garden's autumn apples. I crushed the contents together and put the small case inside the larger, like Russian matryoshka dolls. Partying with sister Fiona's crowd in London before departing, I was unaware that these uneaten apples would, worryingly, upset US Ag & Fish at Miami Customs. In this chaotic way, I was planning to take off from Heathrow for a year of too many adventures, an unwitting, latter-day Johnny Appleseed.

On my last night, I awoke suddenly. Ferry, yes, Ferry, that must be Liverpudlian John's surname, Ferry, John Ferry. "Ferry Cross The Mersey." I knew that had to be the case. Now I have a specific reason to return to Sennen in future, before John stops working his car park summers.

Deep, dark December heralded my departure from Sennen. Trying to conserve my money, I'd decided to hitch-hike to London, cheaper than the train and free, besides. I told myself, it's more interesting to talk to a lorry driver and try to keep him awake on that long journey. I hitch-hiked to Penzance and walked out of town past the railway station, looking down on the London train. A group of Pirates' rugby supporters were warming up for today's match up at Exeter by chanting, "Oggy Oggy Oggy, Oy, Oy, Oy," oggy being a slang term for a pasty. Even Cornwall was nicknamed Oggyland. The tin miners' wives would shout, 'Oggy Oggy Oggy' when delivering pasties to their husbands into the tin mines. Sadly, everyone has now adopted that chant.

I could still remember the mid-sixties when the last steam trains pulled *The Cornish Riviera Express* upcountry to Paddington. The morning stokers used to cook their bacon 'n' eggs on their shovels inside the fire box, the glowing coals brightening their grimy faces. Ah, nostalgia, The Great Western Railway, GWR, known to locals as God's Wonderful Railway.

Whilst hitch-hiking to London, I was considering the Watermen of Hawaii, masters of the water world for sport, earning, cleansing, adventure, a life which ignores pollution and the city. I'd surfed, explored, fished, and earned my living from, with, by, and in the water. For four summers, I'd been a sprite disporting myself in the margins of the sea, a water nymph in a state of limbo between childhood and adulthood. I considered the serious aspects: yes, I had been responsible; I'd had no swimmers' deaths in my four summers at Sennen, however during this last summer, deaths had started to worry me, even on my days off. Now, I'd started worrying – would my replacement cope come '73? Forget worry, boy, you should be terrified – a real adult's adventure starts tomorrow.

I know not all that may be coming,
but be what it will, I'll go to it laughing.
HERMAN MELVILLE, MOBY DICK.

Hairy surfer on a B707 over Sennen cove, Miami next

123

Acknowledgements

To my uni pal Steve Le Duc for careful reading and timely advice, my surfing pal Alastair for his 'historic and heroic' photos, and to my darling daughter Tanya for proofreading the text whilst overlooking my youthful escapades.